EXPERIENCING THE REAL

WITH THE HAWAI'I VISITORS & CONVENTION BUREAU

Book Concept and Author: Peter Rosegg
Editor: Cheryl Chee Tsutsumi
Designer: Angela Wu-Ki
Research Assistants: Jerry Blue, Chris Ching, Linda Hofstedt
Cover Art: Al Furtado

Published and distributed by
Island Heritage Publishing

ISBN 0-89610-382-X

Address orders and correspondence to:

ISLAND HERITAGE
P U B L I S H I N G

94-411 Kōʻaki Street
Waipahu, Hawaiʻi 96797
Telephone: (800) 468-2800
            (808) 564-8800
www.islandheritage.com

Printed in Hong Kong

First edition, first printing, 2001

The information in this book was accurate as of press time. Please note, however, that tour inclusions, content of shows, restaurants' menus, hours for shops and attractions, etc. are subject to change. Before finalizing your plans, it's a good idea to call ahead for the most current information.

EXPERIENCING THE REAL

WITH THE HAWAI'I VISITORS & CONVENTION BUREAU

OVER 100 GREAT DISCOVERIES THROUGHOUT THE ISLANDS OF ALOHA

ISLAND HERITAGE

DEDICATION

"To all those that keep Hawai'i, Hawai'i"

In 1991, the Hawai'i Visitors & Convention Bureau launched Keep It Hawai'i, a program that recognizes, supports and stimulates the efforts of individuals, associations and companies playing a key role in maintaining Hawai'i's cultural values and keeping alive the aloha spirit.

Tony S. Vericella

Each year, a panel of judges carefully reviews each entry, considering, among other factors, its authenticity, historical value, educational value and uniqueness. A letter of reference from a third party who is deemed qualified in the specific category entered must be enclosed with the entry, along with a written statement explaining how the entry helps to Keep It Hawai'i.

Experiencing the Real Hawai'i contains descriptions of over 100 of the finest Keep It Hawai'i entries. As you go through this book and experience our Hawai'i, please remember it is our people who make it a true island Paradise for visitors and residents alike.

This book is dedicated to all of Hawai'i—to everyone whose efforts preserve and perpetuate a culture we all hold so dear.

Tony S. Vericella
President and Chief Executive Officer
Hawai'i Visitors & Convention Bureau

TABLE OF CONTENTS

PRESERVING THE PAST · Mālama Kahiko

- Four Seasons Resort Hualālai · 17
- Hawaii Theatre Center · 18
- Hawaiian Railway Society · 19
- Hilo Downtown Improvement Association · 20
- 'Iolani Palace · 21
- Kukui Heiau Restoration · 22
- Outrigger Wailea Resort · 23
- Outrigger Waikoloa Beach Resort · 24
- Ramsay Museum · 25
- Sheraton Moana Surfrider · 26

PROGRAMS · Huaka'i Alaka'i

- Cultural Heritage Program · 29
- Hawai'i Calls · 30
- Hawai'i Volcano GeoVentures and Project LAVA · 31
- Hawaiian Art and Artifact Project · 32
- Hawaiian EDventure · 33
- Makawehi Sand Dune Walking Tour · 34
- Mākena Nature Walk · 35
- A Sense of Place Program · 36

EVENTS · Nā Hō'ike Kūikawā

- Aloha Boat Days · 39
- Waimea Town Celebration · 40
- Merrie Monarch Festival · 41
- In Celebration of Canoes · 42
- King Kamehameha Celebration · 43
- Prince Lot Hula Festival · 44
- Na Ka Mahina Mālamalama Festival · 45
- Frank B. Shaner Hawaiian Falsetto Contest · 46
- Aloha Festivals · 47
- Hāpuna Beach Prince Hotel Sam Choy Poke Festival · 48
- Princess Ka'iulani Birthday Commemoration · 49
- Annual Hawaiiana Festival · 50
- Christmas at the Hilton · 51
- New Year's at the Sheraton · 52

- O'AHU
- MAUI
- KAUA'I
- LĀNA'I
- HAWAI'I'S BIG ISLAND
- MOLOKA'I
- HAWAI'I AND BEYOND

MARKERS & MONUMENTS   Kia Hoʻomanaʻo

▦ Waikīkī Historic Trail · 55

▦ Nā Lehua Helelei · 56

▦ ▦ Kamehameha the Great Statues · 57

▦ ▦ King Kalākaua Statues · 58

▦ Queen Lydia Liliʻuokalani Statue · 59

▦ Princess Kaʻiulani Statue · 60

▦ Duke Kahanamoku Statue · 61

TOURS   Kaʻapuni

▦ Gay & Robinson Sugar Plantation Tour · 65

▦ Hāhālua Lele · 66

▦ Maui Cave Adventures · 67

▦ Mauka Makai Excursions · 68

▦ Molokaʻi Mule Ride · 69

▦ Senator Fong's Plantation and Gardens · 70

▦ Temptation Tours · 71

▦ Waikīkī Trolley · 72

SPECIAL   Mahele Kūikawā

▦ ▦ ▦ ▦ Billy Fields Masonry · 75

▦ Hawaiʻi Convention Center · 76

▦ Hoʻokipa Aloha Council · 77

▦ The Music of Hawaiʻi · 78

▦ The Queen's Songbook · 79

▦ ▦ ▦ ▦ ▦ ▦
Waikīkī, In the Wake of Dreams · 80

INTERNET   Pūnāewelewele

▦ www.gohawaii.com · 83

▦ www.chinatownhi.com · 84

▦ www.e808.com · 85

▦ www.hawaii.com · 86

▦ www.rodeohawaii.com · 87

▦ OʻAHU   ▦ MAUI   ▦ KAUAʻI   ▦ LĀNAʻI

▦ HAWAIʻI'S BIG ISLAND   ▦ MOLOKAʻI   ▦ HAWAIʻI AND BEYOND

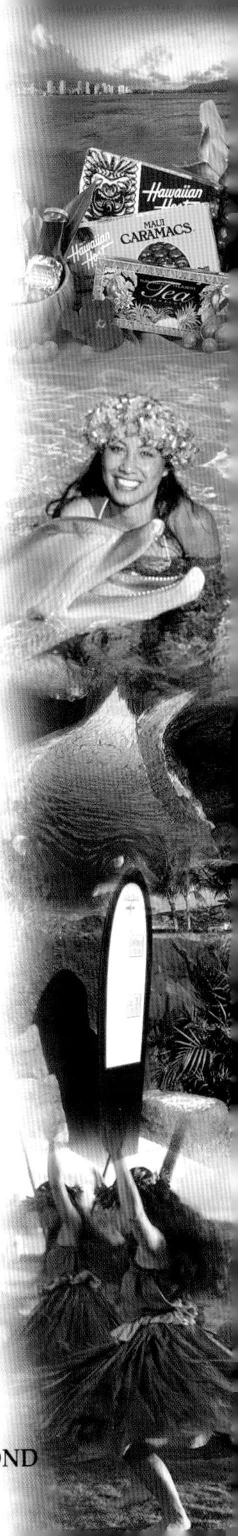

PŌMAIKA'I AWARD

■ ■ ■ ■ ■ ■
Continental Airlines · 91

■ ■ ■ ■ Outrigger Hotels & Resorts · 92

▥ Mountain Apple Company · 93

■ ■ ■ ■ ■ ■
Pleasant Hawaiian Holidays · 94

PROTECTING THE ENVIRONMENT   Mālama 'Āina

■ Chevron Hawai'i · 97
■ Fair Wind Cruises · 98
■ Hilton Waikoloa Village · 99
■ 'Ihilani Resort and Spa · 100

■ Moloka'i Ranch · 101
■ Sheraton Hotels Resource
   Management Program · 102
■ Volcano Art Center · 103

ATTRACTIONS & ACTIVITIES   'Oihana

■ Alexander & Baldwin
   Sugar Museum · 107
■ Bishop Museum · 108
■ Hawai'i Maritime Center · 109
■ Hawai'i Tropical Botanical
   Garden · 110

■ ■ ■ ■ ■ ■
Hawaiian Music Hall of Fame · 111
▥ Maui Ocean Center · 112
■ Polynesian Cultural Center · 113
■ Sea Life Park · 114
■ Waikīkī Aquarium · 115

SHOWS & ENTERTAINMENT   Hō'ike

■ Ali'i Lū'au · 119
■ Drums of Paradise · 120
■ Lobby Bar · 121
▥ Old Lahaina Lū'au · 122

■ Paradise Cove Lū'au · 123
■ Pleasant Hawaiian Hula Show · 124
■ Traditions at Kahalu'u · 125
▥ 'Ulalena · 126

■ O'AHU   ▥ MAUI   ■ KAUA'I   ▥ LĀNA'I

■ HAWAI'I'S BIG ISLAND   ■ MOLOKA'I   ▥ HAWAI'I
                                                       AND BEYOND

STORES · Hale Kū'ai

- Dole Plantation · 129
- Hilo Hattie: The Store of Hawai'i · 130
- Kamehameha Garment Company · 131
- Keālia Ranch Store · 132
- Kings' Shops · 133
- Kwilts 'N Koa · 134
- Mamo Howell · 135
- Martin & MacArthur · 136
- Maui Divers Jewelry Design Center · 137
- Native Books & Beautiful Things · 138
- Nohea Gallery · 139
- Volcano Art Center Gallery · 140

RESTAURANTS · Hale 'Aina

- Alan Wong's Restaurant · 143
- Aloha Mixed Plate · 144
- Don Ho's Island Grill · 145
- Duke's Canoe Club and Barefoot Bar · 146
- Kā'anapali Mixed Plate Restaurant · 147
- Mama's Fish House · 148
- Merriman's and Merriman's Bamboo Bistro · 149
- Tidepools · 150

ACCOMMODATIONS · Hōkele

- Hilton Resorts Hawai'i · 153
  - Hilton Hawaiian Village Beach Resort & Spa
  - Hilton Waikoloa Village
- Outrigger Hotels & Resorts · 156
- Sheraton Hotels Hawai'i · 158
  - Sheraton Moana Surfrider
  - The Royal Hawaiian
  - Sheraton Princess Ka'iulani
  - Sheraton Waikīkī Hotel
- Four Seasons Resort Hualālai · 160
- Hyatt Regency Kaua'i Resort & Spa · 161
- Kīlauea Lodge · 162
- Kona Village Resort · 163
- Moloka'i Ranch Lodge · 164
- Old Wailuku Inn at Ulupono · 165
- Radisson Kaua'i Beach Resort · 166

- O'AHU
- MAUI
- KAUA'I
- LĀNA'I
- HAWAI'I'S BIG ISLAND
- MOLOKA'I
- HAWAI'I AND BEYOND

PREFACE

What makes Hawai'i such a unique place? It's not just its beaches. Many locations have fine beaches, though Hawai'i's silken strands of sand routinely rank on lists of the world's best. It's not just weather, though a year-round summer climate with cooling trade winds makes living—and visiting—here a pleasure. It's not just stunning scenery, great activities and luxurious hotels, though Island resorts have garnered dozens of prestigious awards.

It's not even Hawai'i's friendly people, with their wonderful multiethnic backgrounds.

What Hawai'i claims is a unique culture. Words like aloha and hula, places like Waikīkī and Maui, and items like mu'umu'u and lei are synonymous with Hawai'i alone.

The Hawaiian culture is defined in large part by the aloha spirit. No two people totally agree on the meaning of aloha. Love and concern for everyone—whether they be friends and relatives or strangers—comes immediately to mind, but aloha also encompasses the way Islanders respect the environment, honor the past and plan for the future.

Much more about Hawai'i's culture is unique. Our islands, the most remote landmass in the world, are home to more unique species of plants, animals and fish than any other locale. The Polynesians—who first came here from the Marquesas and Tahiti as early as 300 A.D. and in another large surge in the 12th and 13th centuries—were the greatest sailors on Earth. In double-hulled canoes, these courageous pioneers navigated thousands of miles of open ocean by the wind and stars, settling on Pacific islands more than 2,500 miles from the nearest continent.

When the first Westerners arrived in Hawai'i, they found a proud, intelligent race whose social structure was headed by the ali'i, or those of royal lineage. The Hawaiians were devoted to their gods and families, and respectful of nature and the gifts it provided. For centuries, they had lived a simple life that revolved around fishing and farming.

But change was inevitable, as Westerners (primarily traders, missionaries and businessmen) introduced their language, religion, food, clothing—essentially a new way of life—to the native population. Amid much turmoil, the Hawaiian kingdom, which had endured for a century, was eventually overthrown and the

Islands annexed to the United States. No writer of fiction could pen a story with more color, drama and emotion than this.

Quite simply, there is no place like Hawai'i anywhere on Earth. In 1991, the Hawai'i Visitors & Convention Bureau acknowledged the need to do more to preserve the Islands' rich culture and history. They established the Keep It Hawai'i program to salute those who are working hard to preserve the Hawaiian culture and keep the aloha spirit alive.

Each year, nominations are judged by a panel of distinguished kama'āina (Island residents), including scholars, practitioners of the arts and past winners. From over 100 stellar nominations each year, the judges recognize the best examples in eighteen categories. Entries judged tops in their category receive a Kāhili Award, named for the feather standard that is the symbol of Hawaiian royalty. You will see the distinctive carved wooden Kāhili Awards on display as you visit shops, restaurants, resorts and other establishments throughout the Islands. A feather Kāhili Award is presented annually to the entry deemed Best of Show.

Featuring over 100 of the best Keep It Hawai'i entries from recent years, *Experiencing the Real Hawai'i* was written for two kinds of people—those who live in Hawai'i and those who visit Hawai'i. Did that leave anyone out?

Many visitors are looking for experiences that capture the essence of this special place in the Pacific. Some may spend hours attending lectures or poring over books in libraries, but most prefer receiving information in smaller doses. They like personal encounters with people and places that tell Hawai'i's captivating story. They want to be entertained as well as educated. This book is perfect for such visitors.

It is also intended for local people. Wrapped up in their daily lives, Island residents often overlook the wonderful opportunities they have to strengthen their connection with the things that make Hawai'i such a wonderful place to live.

This guide is not a collection of historic sites, dusty museums or obscure scholarly "artifacts." Opening the possibilities for adventure and discovery, it describes people, places and events that are fun, interesting and accessible. Topics run the gamut, from hotels and stores to attractions and tours that will satiate those seeking a taste of the "real Hawai'i."

Far from an exhaustive look at the Hawaiian culture, *Experiencing the Real Hawai'i* is at most an introduction—a buffet of appetizers, or pūpū, as we call them. So, please, read, sample, savor the offerings.

If you find something you really like, it's not hard to learn more about it. The one thing that the people of Hawai'i like more than living their culture is sharing it.

■ ■ ■

THE HAWAIIAN LANGUAGE

The Hawaiian language is enjoying an auspicious rebirth. During the nineteenth century, Hawaiians were among the most literate people in the world. The Bible was one of the first books translated into Hawaiian, followed by works by Shakespeare and popular novels of the time like *Tarzan*. At one point, there were more than 100 different Hawaiian language newspapers being published throughout the Islands.

Hawaiian was taught in public schools until 1896, three years after the overthrow of the monarchy. A sad decline of the language followed, until in the 1970s it was near extinction. In 1983, a small group of concerned Hawaiian language instructors set out to turn things around.

Modern technology has been used to aid the resurgence of the Hawaiian language. Netscape Navigator has been translated into Hawaiian (it's only the second language after English to be used for this Web browser), and Hawaiian language Web sites and bulletin boards are abundant.

The Pūnana Leo (language nest) movement began in 1983 and now has eleven preschools on Oʻahu, Maui, Kauaʻi and the Big Island of Hawaiʻi, where over 2,000 children are taught entirely in Hawaiian. The schools on Kauaʻi and the Big Island are expanding to instruct kindergarteners through twelfth graders in Hawaiian, with English being the second language. Hawaiian also is taught in elementary and high schools, universities and community classes statewide.

Today, many books and the *Honolulu Advertiser,* one of Hawaiʻi's daily newspapers, use the Hawaiian language's special punctuation marks, which are also used in this book. The ʻokina (glottal stop) looks like a backward apostrophe and is found between some vowels or at the beginning of some words that start with a vowel. It signals a brief pause should come between the syllables, as in "uh-oh."

The kahakō (macron), a line found over some vowels, indicates they should be stressed. Otherwise, vowels are pronounced like this: a like a in above, e like e in bet, i like y in city, o like o in sole, and u like oo in moon.

The Hawaiian language's seven consonants are pronounced much as in English, except w, which is spoken as a v when it appears after an i or e. For example, ʻEwa Beach is pronounced "Eva Beach." You will hear many people call the Islands "Ha-va-ii."

Hawaiian words are sprinkled through the everyday speech of most local residents, along with pidgin from other ethnic groups. Listen carefully and see what words you can catch in conversations with tour guides, hotel concierges, servers at restaurants, store clerks and other Islanders.

Be warned, though, about the malihini (newcomer) who went home convinced that mahalo means "trash." Mahalo actually means "thank you," but the visitor saw it printed on rubbish cans everywhere he went—and just assumed.

HOW TO USE THIS GUIDE

An official guide of the Hawai'i Visitors & Convention Bureau containing over 100 great things to do and places to see, *Experiencing the Real Hawai'i* is designed to be an easy-to-read reference. In the Table of Contents, for example, entries are listed by category (Stores, Restaurants, Shows and Entertainment and so on) and color-coded by island. You can use this book to plan your itinerary in advance, or you can carry it with you to make the most of your Hawai'i experience as you go along.

A few tips are in order. It is always wise to call and confirm that a place is open or an event is occurring before going. Check hours and prices (if applicable), and ask for directions if you need them. It's also a good idea to inquire about parking, recommended attire and other details.

Use Hawai'i's area code 808 with the seven-digit number when calling from out of state or when calling from island to island. Within any island, just dial the seven-digit number.

Finally, a word about getting around. When you ask for directions, instead of the usual compass points, you are most likely to be told to go "mauka" (toward the mountains or inland) or "makai" (toward the ocean). On O'ahu, you may be instructed to go "Diamond Head" (toward the east, where the famous landmark is located) or "'Ewa" (toward the western town of 'Ewa).

Enjoy this book and your stay in Paradise!

Feather lei collection, Outrigger Wailea Resort, Maui.

Hawaiian tattoo demonstration, Four Seasons Resort
Hualālai, Big Island. Photo by John Russell.

Preserving the past is a special challenge on Pacific islands like Hawai'i, born of volcanic eruptions and tossed by waves and occasional storms. Before Western contact, stone was the most
enduring substance, so a low-walled place of worship or a carving made in lava as it hardened takes
on great significance, but may be hard to decipher in later times.

Artistic treasures made of wood, bone or feathers were fragile and short-lived. Those that survived were often taken away by traders, sailors and missionaries to be admired in distant places.
Compared to many parts of the world, Hawai'i's history is relatively brief, spanning less than 2,000
years. Before the Hawaiians had a written language (which was created for them by the missionaries),
they passed their genealogy, family stories and important historical events orally from generation to
generation. Oral traditions are as hard to preserve as grass huts.

In Hawai'i, land is valuable and construction costs are high. Thus, it is almost always cheaper to
tear down and start over (and in the process, build bigger) than it is to restore historical buildings.
That makes the challenge of preservation even greater.

In some cases, preserving the past means restoring the old. In others, it means building or creating something new in age but old in its respect for history. In still other cases, it is finding arts and
crafts and bringing them back to where they can be admired by the descendants of their creators.
Some of the best "historic preservation" is the work of present-day Hawaiian artists and craftspeople
paying homage to the past using modern techniques.

The Hawai'i Visitors & Convention Bureau's Keep It Hawai'i program is all about preserving
the past in a way that is meaningful and useful to the present. The historical preservation category
is open to a wide range of efforts. We explore a few of the best here.

■ FOUR SEASONS RESORT HUALĀLAI

Many hotels in Hawai'i are richly decorated with art from the Islands, Asia or Europe. But one resort claims to have the only hotel collection focused "exclusively" on life in Hawai'i.

The Four Seasons Resort Hualālai on the Big Island's Kona Coast displays 100 original paintings, artifacts, crafts, textiles, photographs and hand-colored prints created from 1775 to the 1950s. A few pieces in its collection were made after statehood, such as re-creations of two mahiole (feather helmets) made by artist Patrick Horimoto with tightly woven 'ie'ie vines and dyes made from kukui nuts. Renowned artist, author and historian Herb Kawainui Kane also created ten heroic paintings detailing life in ancient Hawai'i.

But most of the resort's art and artifacts come from an earlier time. Among the jewels of

The resort's Ka'ūpūlehu Cultural Center is a valuable resource about life in ancient Hawai'i. Photo by Robert Miller.

the collection are a lei niho palaoa, a five-inch walrus ivory hook on a plaited human hair lei estimated to be 175 years old; a full-length tapa robe believed to have been worn by a missionary; a koa wood canoe dating from 1840; and a collection of Hawaiian paddles from the early 1900s.

Artist John Kelly, whose works are displayed in the National Gallery in Washington, is represented by nearly thirty original etchings dating between the 1920s and 1950s. Three of Charles Bartlett's original hand-colored woodcuts from the early 1920s are here as well: the classic *Hawaiian Fisherman, Surfing at Waikīkī* and *Duke Kahanamoku.*

The resort offers visitors a seven-page booklet for a self-guided tour.

Address: 100 Ka'ūpūlehu Drive
Ka'ūpūlehu-Kona, Hawai'i 96740
Phone: 325-8000
Web site: www.fourseasons.com/hualalai

Learning to weave lau hala or pandanus leaves. Photo by John Russell.

■ HAWAII THEATRE CENTER

When it opened in 1922, O'ahu's Hawaii Theatre was heralded as "the pride of the Pacific." Consolidated Amusement Company built it as a showplace for vaudeville, plays, musicals and silent films (in 1929 it became the first theater in the Islands to screen a "talkie").

Now the historic Hawaii Theatre Center is again the place "to see and be seen." A grand center for the performing arts, it is listed on both the state and national registers of historic places.

Restored at a cost of over $22 million over ten years, it is a sumptuous marvel, as exciting

This view from the balcony reveals the splendor of the historic Hawaii Theatre.

to visit empty as when shows fill the stage. From the front of the house, the Corinthian columns, high-domed auditorium, murals and mosaics catch the eye. Unseen at the back of the house is a state-of-the-art lighting and sound system and other excellent facilities, including the Robert Morton Theatre Organ.

Many shows come to the theater, but local audiences love its Hawaiian Friday Nights, which offer the best in authentic popular Island music. After each show, the audience can meet and "talk story" with the musicians at a post-concert gathering in the neighboring Chinatown Gateway Park.

A one-hour guided tour highlighting the theater's history, art, architecture and restoration is scheduled every Tuesday at 11:00 A.M. Tour times and days are subject to change, so be sure to call to confirm specifics before going.

Address: 1130 Bethel Street
Honolulu, Hawai'i 96813
Phone: 528-0506 (box office)
Web site: www.hawaiitheatre.com

■ HAWAIIAN RAILWAY SOCIETY

At one time, trains were in operation on every Hawaiian island except Niʻihau and Kahoʻolawe. Seven public carrier railroads ran on the four main islands. During the sugar industry's heyday from the 1860s to the 1940s, forty-seven plantations had private railway systems with up to nine locomotives each. The U.S. military also had its own rail system.

**Take a tour of the ʻEwa coast in Oʻahu's last train.
Photo by Mark Brueshaber.**

The history of Hawaiian railroading is now mostly retold in songs and hulas, but in 1970, the Hawaiian Railway Society was established to preserve what remained of the Islands' railroad history. This educational, nonprofit organization got the remaining fifteen-mile stretch of Oʻahu track from ʻEwa to Nānākuli on the state and national registers of historic places, and has so far rebuilt about seven miles of it.

Three vintage diesel locomotives have been renewed to working status, and several steam locomotives have been cosmetically restored. A parlor car that sugar and rail baron Benjamin Dillingham rode to inspect the 170-plus miles of his railway line track around Oʻahu has been restored to look as it did in the 1890s, and is put into service on the second Sunday of each month.

Hawaiian Railway offers two narrated ninety-minute tours at 12:30 and 2:30 P.M. each Sunday. Charters are available other days.

**Address: 91-1001 Renton Road
ʻEwa Beach, Hawaiʻi 96706
Phone: 681-5461
Web site: http://members.aol.com/
hawaiianrr/index.html**

On Maui, the Lahaina Kāʻanapali & Pacific Railroad offers six round-trips a day. Pioneer Mill, the last plantation in West Maui, closed in 1999 after 104 years in operation, but the Sugar Cane Train still steams along the edge of its 6,000 now-fallow acres. To complement its tour, which features a singing conductor, Lahaina Kāʻanapali & Pacific Railroad hopes to one day build a sugarcane museum.

**Address: 975 Limahana Place
Lahaina, Hawaiʻi 96761
Phone: 667-6851
Web site: thesupersites.com/sugarcanetrain/**

■ HILO DOWNTOWN IMPROVEMENT ASSOCIATION

While downtown Honolulu has largely gone high-rise, downtown Hilo on the Big Island houses Hawai'i's largest core of historic buildings. Some date back to the 1870s and display a unique architectural mix. You can see art deco and renaissance revival influences mixed among ramshackle tin-roofed wooden buildings.

This commercial photographer's studio on Haili Street stands on the same site and is an exact reproduction of one of the first houses built in downtown Hilo. Photo by Boone Morrison.

Hilo gets a lot of rainfall and twice in the last half century has been devastated by tsunamis or tidal waves. In 1946, an Alaskan earthquake triggered a tsunami that sent fifty-foot waves over Hilo, destroying buildings and killing nearly 100 people. In 1960, a tsunami originating off the coast of Chile hit Hilo with three successive waves, killing sixty-one and causing $23 million in damage.

With all the destruction that has occurred in Hilo, it is amazing that it remains such a historic preserve. The Hilo Downtown Improvement Association has been at the center of efforts to restore and revitalize the downtown area. It offers a pamphlet so you can guide yourself on a walk around the historic town.

The tour includes Kalākaua Park; the Taishoji Soto Mission, established by Zen Buddhists in 1913; and the art deco Palace Theater, built in 1925 and now being restored as a movie theater and community arts center.

Dating back to the early 1900s, the Hawai'i Telephone Company building was designed by C.W. Dickey, father of Hawaiian regional architecture. The Fire and Water Exhibit at the Historic Kress Building, constructed in 1932 in art deco style, features photos of the tsunamis, volcanic eruptions and earthquakes that have shaped the life of Hilo.

Along Kamehameha Avenue, you can find one-of-a-kind stores offering local crafts and artwork, distinctive designer aloha wear and vintage Island treasures as well as excellent restaurants. Every Wednesday and Sunday, the Hilo Farmers Market brings one corner of Mamo Street alive. Shoppers scoop up bargains on merchandise ranging from locally made arts and crafts to delicious baked goods to tropical fruits and flowers grown in the Big Island's fertile fields.

Address: 38 Haili Street
Hilo, Hawai'i 96720
Phone: 935-8850
Web site: www.downtownhilo.com

'IOLANI PALACE

'Iolani Palace on O'ahu served its regal purpose for only eleven years. The cornerstone was laid on the very last day of 1879, under the direction of King Kalākaua, on the site of an older, smaller palace, also called 'Iolani, which means royal hawk and was one of the given names of King Kamehameha IV.

Built in a style called American Florentine, the new 'Iolani Palace was equipped with flush toilets and Hawai'i's first telephones and electric lights. Construction was completed in December 1882, and Kalākaua held court there until his death on January 20, 1891. His sister, Queen Lili'uokalani, ruled only two years until January 17, 1893, when American businessmen backed by U.S. Marines overthrew the monarchy.

In 1895, two years after the overthrow of the monarchy and a quickly suppressed rebellion to restore her throne, Lili'uokalani spent eight months under house arrest in a second-floor room of the palace.

The palace survived seventy-five years of use and abuse, including serving as the capital of the republic, territory and finally state of Hawai'i until 1969. The Friends of 'Iolani Palace then initiated a massive restoration project, and the palace was officially reopened in 1978. In fact, the restoration is ongoing as The Friends are continually searching for original furnishings.

A visit to the palace inspires anyone with an interest in history. Forty-five-minute guided tours begin every fifteen minutes between 9:00 A.M. and 2:15 P.M. Tuesday through Saturday.

'Iolani Palace was the residence of King Kalākaua and Queen Lili'uokalani, Hawai'i's last reigning monarchs.
Photo by HVCB-Chuck Painter

Most impressive are the three-story koa wood stairwell and the magnificent Throne Room, with silk brocatelle thrones in place.

In November 2000, Phase I of the 'Iolani Palace Galleries opened in the palace basement. Among the ancient and late monarchy regalia on view are the Crown Jewels of Hawai'i, royal feather capes, personal jewelry of the queens, and royal orders presented and received by King Kalākaua. The Galleries may be visited without reservations, however, reservations should be made for the guided tour of the palace.

Hawaiian sovereignty rallies, as well as many other ceremonies, often take place on the palace grounds. Today, governors of Hawai'i are sworn in at the Coronation Pavilion, and every Friday at noon (except in August) the Royal Hawaiian Band presents a concert here.

Address: 364 South King Street
Honolulu, Hawai'i 96813
Phone: 522-0832
Web site: http://openstudio.hawaii.edu/iolani

■ KUKUI HEIAU RESTORATION

In ancient days, kukui oil burning in large stone lamps at Kukui Heiau on Kaua'i showed Hawaiian canoe paddlers crossing from O'ahu where to find the safety of Wailua Bay and the river beyond. Wailua was then the home of royalty and seat of political power on Kaua'i.

Kukui Heiau is located on Kaua'i's Alakukui Point but until recently, the ancient Hawaiian place of worship was overgrown and its stone walls were barely visible. Listed on both the national and state registers of historic places, the heiau dates from the second migration of Polynesians to Hawai'i, somewhere between 1100 and 1400 A.D.

In ancient times, stone lamps lit with kukui nut oil at Kukui Heiau led canoe voyagers to a safe anchorage at Wailua Bay.

In February 1999, Outrigger Hotels & Resorts took over management of the Lae nani Resort Condominium, on whose grounds the heiau stands. Gregg Enright, general manager of the resort, set out to restore the sacred site with the help of Outrigger, the state's Department of Land and Natural Resources, and Lester Calipjo, owner of GK Landscaping, who was hired to do the restoration.

Three months later, the heiau, which measures seventy by 230 feet, was restored to a condition "suitable to its importance," as the archaeologists put it. Visitors to the beautiful beach at the mouth of the Wailua River can see the heiau's walls and wander respectfully inside. A metal plaque, donated by the owners of Lae nani Resort, now marks the site. If you'd like to learn more, stop by the resort's office, where you can pick up a free brochure that expands on the heiau's historical and cultural significance.

Address: 410 Papaloa Road
Kapa'a, Hawai'i 96746
Phone: 822-4938
Web site: www.outrigger.com

■ OUTRIGGER WAILEA RESORT

Outrigger Hotels & Resorts spent over $25 million to renovate this lovely, twenty-five-year-old oceanfront Maui hotel, determined to give it a "Hawaiian sense of place."

You will notice this everywhere, from the moment you enter the lobby. Take an extra moment to find the resort's Hawaiian feather lei collection. Outrigger commissioned two leading feather lei artisans—Aunty Mary Lou Kekuewa and her daughter, Paulette Kahalepuna—to create the gorgeous pieces. The names of Hawaiian deities, guardian spirits, ali'i (royalty) and chiefs unique to Maui inspired the creation of feather lei in accordance with ancient traditions.

Move to the Lokelani Ballroom, where dramatic floor-to-ceiling murals depicting life in ancient Hawai'i surround you. The murals illustrate a traditional land division called ahupua'a, which extended from the uplands to the beach. It contained all the resources that were needed to sustain life in old Hawai'i.

The Outrigger Wailea commissioned artist Ronny Lynn of the Lāna'i Arts Program to paint the murals. The ballroom was often booked during the year-and-a-half it took for Lynn to complete the project, but guests loved

A table doubles as a display case for a beautiful selection of feather lei in the Outrigger Wailea Resort's lobby.

seeing the work in progress. Blessed June 12, 1998, the murals also serve as a backdrop to the hotel's Ho'olōkahi cultural program, which teaches visitors basket weaving, lei making and other Hawaiian arts.

Address: 3700 Wailea Alanui Drive
Wailea, Hawai'i 96753
Phone: 879-1922
Web site: www.outrigger.com

■ OUTRIGGER WAIKOLOA BEACH RESORT

The Outrigger Waikoloa Beach is located on the shores of the Big Island's historic 'Anaeho'omalu Bay, a protected cove with a golden sand beach once reserved for Hawaiian royalty. Adjoining the beach is a placid pond fed by a rare natural spring. This pond was used to cultivate mullet to feed visiting kings and chiefs,

The canoe *Kaimalino* and Herb Kāne's striking painting, *HMS Discovery Off Waikoloa, 1793* draw attention in the hotel's lobby.

and it's easy to see how 'Anaeho'omalu, which literally means "restricted mullet," got its name.

Outrigger Hotels & Resorts spent over $26 million to renovate the aging Waikoloa property and to elevate it to a standard that matched its stunning location. The hotel commissioned esteemed Big Island artist, author and historian Herb Kawainui Kāne to create a mural for the lobby. Known for his interest in ships and voyaging canoes, he created a forty-foot painting of Captain George Vancouver's ship, HMS *Discovery,* sailing into 'Anaeho'omalu Bay for the first time in 1793.

Sailing out to meet the ship is a Hawaiian chief's double-hulled canoe. In the distance are the majestic peaks of Hualālai, Mauna Loa and snow-capped Mauna Kea.

Look closely and you will see the Kohala Coast in the painting looks different than it does today. Kane portrayed the hills as lush and green, as they were before grazing cattle and the lava flows of 1801 and 1859 destroyed much of the vegetation.

In front of the mural is a 110-year-old koa wood outrigger canoe named *Kaimalino* or calm sea, a focal point for lectures for guests and staff. Together, the canoe and the mural convey Ke 'Ano Wa'a, The Outrigger Way, the locally owned resort chain's guide to hospitality and Hawaiian preservation.

Address: 69-275 Waikoloa Beach Drive
Waikoloa, Hawai'i 96738
Phone: 886-6789
Web site: www.outrigger.com

▣ RAMSAY MUSEUM

Preserving Hawai'i's past takes many forms. Sometimes it is an architect restoring a beautiful old building; sometimes it is an artist who preserves the same building on paper.

Ramsay, who uses simply one name, is such an artist. Her detailed pen-and-ink drawings have captured the historic treasures of Hawai'i, from old Kōloa town on the island of Kaua'i to the ornate facade of the Alexander & Baldwin Building on Bishop Street in downtown Honolulu. Ramsay purchased and restored the Tan Sing building on Smith Street in Honolulu's Chinatown and opened a gallery there that was one of the first to revive downtown Honolulu as an arts center.

Ramsay, who has been named a "Living Treasure of Hawai'i," has nurtured other artists as well, providing over 200 of them with

Ever-changing exhibits spotlight the work of new and established Hawai'i artists. Photo by Gary Hoffheimer.

public exposure in her galleries and launching many now-flourishing careers in art. She formed the Ramsay Foundation to advance art in the Islands, and its collection contains several hundred works by Hawai'i's premier artists.

Now, Ramsay Museum continues to provide a venue for other performances and gatherings, such as an exhibition called *Chinese Families in Hawai'i* and a launch party for the book, *The Story of the Scots in Hawai'i*. That's no surprise, really, since Ramsay is particularly proud of her Scottish heritage. In 1989, she was the first woman to be named "Scot of the Year" by the Caledonian Society of Hawai'i.

Address: 1128 Smith Street
Honolulu, Hawai'i 96813
Phone: 537-2787
Hours: 10:00 A.M. TO 5:00 P.M. Monday through Friday; 10:00 A.M. TO 4:00 P.M. Saturday
Web site: www.ramsaymuseum.org

This pretty courtyard is a hidden delight at Ramsay Gallery. Photo by Gary Hoffheimer.

■ SHERATON MOANA SURFRIDER

Day and night, an alluring lady on Kalākaua Avenue in Waikīkī beckons to visitors from all over the world. She is "The First Lady of Waikīkī," better known as the Sheraton Moana Surfrider. Although the resort has added wings over the years, the original 1901 Moana is still there, displaying the renewed splendor of a $50-million face-lift completed in 1989.

The beaux-arts architecture flaunts tall columns, an intricate facade, broad verandas and an elegant porte cochere. Up the Grand Staircase on the second floor is the Historical Room, the only one of its kind in a Waikīkī resort. This mini-museum displays room keys, china, brochures, clothing and other memorabilia dating back to the turn of the century.

There's a video on the legendary beachboys of Waikīkī and the revival of surfing, as well as an exhibit on "Hawai'i Calls," the radio show that was broadcast at the Banyan Veranda from 1935 to 1975. Peek through the

The Historical Room provides a peek of life in Hawai'i at the turn of the century.

lens of an antique camera to check out a panoramic photo taken offshore in 1901, showing the "new" Moana Hotel. Look for photos of the famous Moana Pier, built in 1890 as part of a private estate. It jutted one-fourth of a mile into the water to a small pavilion where musicians often gathered for impromptu concerts.

When it was demolished in 1930, *Paradise of the Pacific,* the forerunner of today's *Honolulu* magazine, described the pier as a place where "a thousand romances have begun and perhaps as many dissolved."

The Historical Room is always open. In addition, free tours are offered at 11:00 A.M. and 5:00 P.M. Monday through Friday. You can sign up for a tour at the hotel's concierge desk.

This is how the Moana Hotel and its famous pier looked prior to 1930.

**Address: 2365 Kalākaua Avenue
Honolulu, Hawai'i 96815
Phone: 922-3111
Web site: www.sheraton-hawaii.com**

Molten lava creates intriguing patterns, Big Island.
Photo by Janet Babb, Project LAVA.

Puʻuhonua o Hōnaunau on the Big Island harbors many treasures
from Hawaiʻi's past, including three heiau, places of worship.
Photo by Hawaiian EDventures.

Do you have an appetite for adventure? Are you the independent sort who enjoys trying different things? If so, the discoveries in this chapter are for you.

Some require a little more effort right from the start. For example, if you want to visit the Hawaiian Music Hall of Fame you will have to find it. With no permanent home, the exhibition moves from place to place. And although the Waikīkī Trolley's friendly drivers will tell you where their routes go, you will have to decide when to jump off and explore.

TheBus, Oʻahu's public transportation system, is the best deal for exploring the island. One-way fares cost just $1.50 for adults and seventy-five cents for kids. The $15 Discovery Pass aimed at visitors allows unlimited rides for four consecutive days. For more information, call 848-5555 or peruse the Web site, www.thebus.org.

Whether sightseeing by public bus or via rental car, you can be your own tour guide. Armed with a good map, a "drive guide" magazine from the rental car agency or Richard Sullivan's excellent book, *Driving and Discovering Hawaiʻi,* you'll do fine. Don't worry about making wrong turns. After all, on an island you can't venture too far away from your destination.

Most of the programs in this chapter are designed for visitors, but some are truly off the tourist track. The longer immersion programs may not be for everyone. But if you like to immerse yourself in a place and make personal contact with the people who live there, these options can offer the experiences of a lifetime.

■ CULTURAL HERITAGE PROGRAM
KING KAMEHAMEHA'S KONA
BEACH HOTEL

In the heart of Kailua-Kona town on the Big Island, King Kamehameha's Kona Beach Hotel sits on the site of Kamakahonu (the eye of the turtle), once the residence of Kamehameha the Great and the first capital of the Hawaiian kingdom he unified.

The hotel created its Cultural Heritage Program to honor its historic location and heritage. On display in the lobby, whose walls gleam with koa wood, are antiques and authentic reproductions of items used daily by the ancient Hawaiians. Also featured are oil portraits of Nā Mō'ī O Hawai'i, Hawaiian Royalty, proud additions to the hotel's historical tribute.

In 1812, King Kamehameha rededicated a temple at Kamakahonu that may date back to the fifteenth century, and dedicated it to Lono, the god of agriculture and prosperity. The temple was known as Ahu'ena Heiau (the burning altar).

An older hotel stood at this site and when it was demolished, the new one that replaced it was set back from the bay. The heiau was again restored in 1975 by David Kahelemauna Roy, Jr., the honored Kahu (guardian) of the temple, with the support of the Bishop Museum.

As you visit this National Historic Site, note the sacred temple drum created as part of the restoration after an original temple drum

A canoe carrying Islanders representing Hawaiian Royalty approaches the restored heiau at Kamakahonu.

housed at the Bishop Museum. You can take a self-guided tour through the lobby and grounds of King Kamehameha's Kona Beach Hotel at any time with the help of an informational brochure, or you can sign up for a free thirty-minute guided tour every weekday afternoon. Check with the hotel's concierge for the specific time and meeting place.

You also can visit the Kūlana Room in the hotel lobby, where the staff of Kūlana Huli Honua (Foundation for the Search for Wisdom), led by Kahu David Roy and his daughter, Mikahala Roy, offer a regular series of classes for guests and Island residents alike. Call 327-0123 for information about classes and special tours.

Address: 75-5660 Palani Road
Kailua-Kona, Hawai'i 96740
Phone: 329-2911
Web site: www.konabeachhotel.com

■ ■ ■ HAWAI'I CALLS: MUSIC, HISTORY, CULTURE AND CHERISHED PLACES OF THE ISLANDS
PACIFIC ISLANDS INSTITUTE

Music is often called a universal language, and Hawaiian music has a huge following around the world. More than entertainment, it is a door to Hawai'i's unique culture. Open it, and you'll be amazed at what you'll discover.

Lei-making classes enhance the Hawai'i Calls experience.

That is the basic idea behind "Hawai'i Calls: Music, History, Culture and Cherished Places of the Islands," an educational program developed by the Pacific Islands Institute in conjunction with Hawai'i Pacific University and currently offered through Elderhostel, Inc. It uses oli (chants), mele (songs) and hīmeni (hymns) as a way to explore Hawai'i's culture, history, natural beauty, values and language.

This is an all-inclusive, two-week program that travels to three islands—O'ahu, Maui and Kaua'i—for music and hula performances, lectures by Hawaiian cultural experts and field trips to inspirational places. Nearly twenty instructors—including leading Island performers, artisans, teachers and academicians—ensure the authenticity of the program. Tour leaders who accompany the group from beginning to end make certain everything runs smoothly.

The Pacific Islands Institute organizers have been conducting similar programs for twenty years, so they know what they are doing. They have handled over 800 groups in Hawai'i and 200 more in Polynesia and Melanesia. Such tours have been planned for Hawai'i Pacific University, the National Parks Conservation Association, American Hawai'i Cruises, and a number of other clubs and organizations. Similar tours can be customized for other groups.

Clearly, this sort of immersion in Hawaiian culture is not everyone's cup of poi. For those who want to delve deeply into the culture, guided by some of its most committed and caring keepers, Hawai'i Calls is among the best ways to do it. Its glowing testimonials and increasing number of participants attest to that.

Address: 354 Uluniu Street, Suite 408
Kailua, Hawai'i 96734
Phone: 262-8942
Web site: www.pac-island.com

■ HAWAI'I VOLCANO GEOVENTURES AND PROJECT LAVA (Learning About Volcanic Activity)

Two million people visit Hawai'i Volcanoes National Park on the Big Island each year. The average visitor spends about four hours there, marveling at craters, cinder cones, steaming ground cracks and other volcanic features.

For many, that is enough. However, if you want a more in-depth experience, here's how you can get it.

Hawai'i Volcano GeoVentures offers guided geologic adventures on Kīlauea Volcano. The tours and hikes are customized for individuals, families, students, photographers and special interest groups.

Janet Babb, a geologist/educator and long-time volunteer at the Hawaiian Volcano Observatory, leads the geoventures. She also developed Project LAVA (Learning About Volcanic Activity), a weeklong program for elementary and secondary schoolteachers. Volcanic eruptions fuel the imagination of almost everyone, so teachers can use the study of volcanoes to get their students interested in science.

Since it began in 1995, Project LAVA has drawn teachers from the United States, England, Egypt, Canada, Germany and Australia, and has grown to four sessions a year. Each class is limited to twenty participants, who stay in the historic Volcano House hotel on the rim of Kīlauea's summit crater.

Teachers learn about volcanic processes, photograph Kīlauea's stark landscape, explore

Sunrise over a lava flow, Big Island.
Photo by Janet Babb, Project LAVA.

lava tubes and, if they are lucky, witness the creation of new land as molten lava pours into the sea. They learn about Pele, the Hawaiian goddess of fire, and watch demonstrations of traditional hula that recount legends about her. They also explore the Big Island's lush rain forests, black sand beaches and other natural features.

Class participants can earn academic credit by participating in the program, but most teachers say their biggest reward is the look of awe and excitement on their students' faces when they share the adventures they experienced on Hawai'i's active volcano.

Address: P.O. Box 816
Volcano, Hawai'i 96785
Phone: 985-9901
Web sites: www.projectlava.com/geoventures
(Hawai'i Volcano GeoVentures)
www.projectlava.com (Project LAVA)

Four Project LAVA sessions are conducted during the year, typically one in late June, two in July and one in September.

◼ HAWAIIAN ART AND ARTIFACT PROJECT
KAUA'I MARRIOTT RESORT & BEACH CLUB

Hawaiian trivia question: What did Prince Kūhiō name his koa wood canoe? And, for extra credit, where can you see that canoe today? Is that your final answer?

Prince Kūhiō, affectionately known as Prince Cupid, named his sleek, graceful outrigger canoe, *Princess.* Dramatically displayed in the lobby of the Kaua'i Marriott Resort & Beach Club, it is the centerpiece of the Hawaiian Art and Artifact Project, a $300,000 initiative to create a truly Hawaiian environment at the hotel. You can stroll around at your leisure to view the treasures; there is no charge.

As you enter the Kaua'i Marriott, you are greeted by two kāhili (feather standards) in purple, Kaua'i's official island color. They were created by master crafters Mary Louise Kekuewa and her daughter, Paulette Kahalepuna, and presented to the resort with a proper Hawaiian blessing.

Carved wooden ki'i (image).

The handsome outrigger canoe *Princess* once belonged to Prince Kūhiō.

You'll see many other displays as you roam the resort, among them decorated ipu (bottle gourd) drums, by noted Island craftsman No'eau Penner; hula instruments by kumu (teacher) Patrick Choi displayed on a beautiful stretch of Colleen Kimura's hand-screened fabric dyed purple, of course; and a collection of Hawaiian weapons, including a dagger, spears and shark-tooth club created by Big Island artist Ski Kwiatkowski.

One of the highlights of the Hawaiian Art and Artifact Project is also one of its oldest pieces—a length of kapa (tapa) that dates back over a century. The watermarkings on this fine example of bark cloth, called hālau 'upena (meshes of a net), were a favorite design of the people who lived in fishing villages on Kaua'i, leading experts to believe the kapa is "homegrown."

**Address: 3610 Rice Street
Līhue, Hawai'i 96766
Phone: 245-5050
Web site: www.marriotthotels.com/marriott/
LIHHI/home.html**

■ HAWAIIAN EDVENTURE

Created by the University of Hawaiʻi at Hilo in collaboration with Destination Hilo, Hawaiian EDventure is an ongoing travel education and cultural program designed for visitors from eight to eighty years old.

One EDventure program, "Going Back to Our Roots" (or E Hoʻi Mai E Ke Kumu, in Hawaiian), enables participants to learn about Hawaiʻi and its culture through the lives of knowledgeable kūpuna (elders) who teach treasured skills such as lau hala (pandanus leaf) weaving, lei making, woodcarving and playing the ʻukulele. They also pass on traditions and legends of old Hawaiʻi that help to perpetuate the culture.

The diverse Big Island serves as the background when EDventure brings the classroom into the field. With settings like Waipiʻo Valley, where Papa John Auwae explains the importance of taro; Puʻuhonua O Hōnaunau (Place of Refuge), where Kumu David Roy and Mikahala Roy "talk story" about Hawaiʻi's past; and Parker Ranch, where real paniolo (cowboys) describe their lives and homes on the range, the Big Island serves as the greatest living laboratory in the world.

Hawaiian EDventure combines education and recreation to provide hands-on programs in marine biology, vulcanology, geology, astronomy, Hawaiiana, health, wellness and the fine arts. It offers a way for people from around the world to connect with renowned scientists, artists, musicians, teachers and business professionals in the Islands.

These are some of the best examples of new travel notions like edu-tourism and eco-tourism around. The interactions between local elders and visitors, young and old, offer some of the most memorable experiences in the Hawaiian EDventure program. "Designer" programs also are available to meet the specific educational and cultural needs of groups, professional organizations, schools, clubs and families coming to Hawaiʻi.

**Address: University of Hawaiʻi
at Hilo Conference Center
200 West Kāwili Street
Hilo, Hawaiʻi 96720
Phone: 974-7555
Web site: conference.uhh.hawaii.edu/edventure.html**

Hawaiian EDventure participants get a close-up look at an intriguing marine creature.

■ MAKAWEHI SAND DUNE
WALKING TOUR
HYATT REGENCY KAUA'I RESORT & SPA

The Hyatt Regency Kaua'i Resort & Spa stands on Po'ipū Beach along lovely Keoneloa Bay, near the Makawehi sand dunes, perhaps the most extensively excavated archaeological sites on the island of Kaua'i. Every other Monday, the resort and the Kaua'i Historical Society offer a guided walking tour of the dunes, which passes heiau (places of worship) and fishing altars, boundary walls, and house and burial sites. The dunes harbor fossils and artifacts that vividly tell the geological, biological and anthropological history of the area.

The Makawehi sand dunes rank among Hawai'i's most significant archaeological sites.

Archaeologically speaking, the site is still "alive." Visitors are advised to watch for places where winds and shifting sands may have uncovered new remains so the state's Historic Preservation Division can be notified to document them.

The Hyatt Regency Kaua'i Resort & Spa also commissioned a video, *The Land of Pā'ā: Past and Future,* which provides a glimpse into the history, culture and spiritual power of the ahupua'a (land division) where the hotel is located. In the video, kūpuna (elders), kumu (teachers) and archaeologists share their insights about the surrounding Po'ipū and Kōloa areas.

For example, we learn that the name of the area is believed to be a combination of pā (enclosure) and a'ā, (rough, coarse lava). Together, Pā'ā means a rocky, dry place.

The resort uses *The Land of Pā'ā: Past and Future* to train new employees, believing that if they develop an interest in and respect for the workplace, it will inspire them to share, from which the true sense of ho'okipa (hospitality) and aloha (love and goodwill) can flow.

Address: 1571 Po'ipū Road
Kōloa, Hawai'i 96756
Phone: 742-1234
Hours: Every other Monday, 9:00 A.M.
Web site: www.kauai-hyatt.com

▦ MĀKENA NATURE WALK
MAUI PRINCE HOTEL

Mākena on the island of Maui is one of those fabled Hawaiian places. Here Pele, the tempestuous Hawaiian fire goddess, is said to have dallied with the handsome Chief Lohiau. And it was here that King Kalākaua came whenever he needed to escape the demanding affairs of state in Honolulu.

The Maui Prince Hotel created its free self-guided Mākena Nature Walk to weave together the history and beauty of its spectacular location. The quarter-mile tour of the hotel's grounds packs in a lot of information. You can enjoy the walk at your own pace, spending as much time as you want at well-marked stops that are described in a full-color booklet.

What's unusual is the small backpack you'll receive, on loan, to take on the tour. Arrows in the booklet tell you when you are to reach into the bag and what you are to pull out. The backpack is filled with surprises.

At Stop #3, for instance, you are instructed to find the bag of birdseed and then ring the bell

The Mākena Nature Walk showcases the beauty of Maui's southern coast.

on the post. "Once you start spreading the birdseed, you should attract some of our feathered kamaʻāina (Island residents)," you'll read in the booklet. "Pictured here are some of the birds most frequently seen. How many can you spot?"

Expect many more wonderful surprises. The word "interactive" is tossed around a lot these days, but here is a tour that truly is interactive—and it doesn't even require a computer!

Address: 5400 Mākena Alanui
Mākena, Hawaiʻi 96753
Phone: 874-1111
Web site: www.princehawaii.com

■ A SENSE OF PLACE PROGRAM
THE RITZ-CARLTON, KAPALUA

When digging began to build The Ritz-Carlton, Kapalua in 1987, the resting place of more than 2,000 Hawaiians who lived from 850 A.D. to the early 1800s was unearthed near Honokahua Bay. Work stopped until the bones could be reburied, and the entire hotel was redesigned and moved inland.

On the State Register of Historic Places, the Honokahua Preservation Site is now reserved for native Hawaiian ceremonial and religious practices. The burial mound is carpeted in lush grass and bordered by a native hau hedge. The sacred site also includes a preserved portion of the sixteenth-century Alaloa or King's Trail, a footpath that once encircled the island of Maui.

Each Friday, guests and visitors to The Ritz-Carlton, Kapalua are invited to attend A Sense of Place, a complimentary presentation led by the hotel's Hawaiian Cultural Adviser, Clifford Nae'ole. Born and raised on Maui, Nae'ole is a member of the Maui-Lāna'i Island Burial Council, which has been entrusted to care for any skeletal remains or artifacts that are discovered on the islands of Maui and Lāna'i.

During the program, Nae'ole discusses the history of the Honokahua Preservation Site and screens the film *Then There Were None*, which examines the plight of the Native Hawaiians from 1778 until present day. Following a ques-

Clifford Nae'ole teaches visitors about the historical and cultural significance of the Honokahua Preservation Site.

tion-and-answer session, Nae'ole takes the group to The Ritz-Carlton, Kapalua's māla lā'au lapa'au (medicinal herb garden), which yields a variety of plants that are being used by practitioners of both modern Western medicine and ancient Polynesian healing techniques. Nae'ole describes the plants' uses and explains how the ancient Hawaiians achieved wellness through spiritual and physical means.

After spending an enlightening hour-and-a-half with the knowledgeable Nae'ole, participants are on their way to developing a "sense of place," or, in Nae'ole's words, "a true understanding of what Hawai'i is."

Address: One Ritz-Carlton Drive
Lahaina, Hawai'i 96761
Phone: 669-6200
Hours: 10:00 A.M. Friday
Web site: www.celebrationofthearts.org/
hawaiian.html

The Aloha Festivals Royal Court arrive in Waikīkī aboard
the sailing canoe *Hōkūleʻa*. Photo by Bob Abraham.

A colorful parade along Front Street is one of the highlights
of the annual Celebration of Canoes in Lahaina, Maui.

Hawai'i's calendars are chock-full of events and festivals. With good weather year round and a naturally sociable attitude, Islanders will take advantage of any excuse to get together and have a good time.

Several festivals in Hawai'i now have an international flair, including the Honolulu Festival, which brings in thousands of visitors from Japan, and the French Festival, which spotlights fashions, food, music and art from that culturally sophisticated locale. Following in the footsteps of the Taste of Honolulu (the annual fund-raiser for Easter Seals that brings specialties from dozens of top O'ahu restaurants to the grounds of the Honolulu Civic Center), towns on the Neighbor Islands have developed their own "taste of" benefits for worthy charities.

In addition to the standard national holidays, Hawai'i observes several state holidays such as Kamehameha Day, Kūhiō Day, May Day (which is known as "Lei Day" here) and Admissions Day (celebrating the day Hawai'i was officially admitted into the Union). In the Islands, there's at least one big celebration planned every month of the year.

Arranged chronologically, the events in this chapter are special in that they help keep Hawaiian culture and tradition alive. As usual, the list is by no means complete. But it does cover a wide range, from events dating back over a century to those that started only a few years ago. Some are fancy and expensive to produce; others about as down-home as you can get, meaning T-shirts, shorts and "rubbah slippahs" are appropriate attire. As always, call the organizers or peruse the Web sites for the latest information on dates, times and admission prices.

■ ALOHA BOAT DAYS
ALOHA TOWER MARKETPLACE

Few things will get old-timers in Hawaiʻi misty-eyed like the mention of the boat days of yesteryear. It is hard to imagine how exciting the arrival of a passenger ship was in the days before jets shrunk travel time between Hawaiʻi and the Mainland.

Today, you can relive that nostalgic time through Aloha Boat Days, free events that welcome visiting cruise ships as they arrive in

Arriving cruise ships receive a warm Aloha Boat Days welcome at Honolulu Harbor, complete with streamers.

Honolulu Harbor or bid them a fond aloha ʻoe (farewell) as they depart. Volunteers from the community established Aloha Boat Days in January 1999, and ever since then the program has shared Hawaiʻi's warm hospitality with every cruise ship that drops anchor in Honolulu.

All the activities take place in Honolulu Harbor and at the landmark Aloha Tower and Aloha Tower Marketplace. There are two regularly scheduled Boat Days every week. One takes place Saturday nights, when American Classic Voyages' ms *Patriot* leaves for a seven-day cruise around the state, and the other happens Thursday afternoons, when the SS *Independence* continues on its weeklong inter-island cruise, which launches Sunday from its home port in Kahului, Maui. Starting in December, 2001 Norwegian Cruise Line's *Norwegian Star* will be homeported in Hawaiʻi, and will enjoy its own Boat Days celebration each weekend. Check the Web site provided below for the arrival times of other ocean liners that call at Honolulu Harbor throughout the year.

A typical Aloha Boat Days event features the fireboat, *Moku ʻAhi*, shooting towering fountains of water as ships enter and depart the harbor; a helicopter circling the ship and showering tropical flowers upon her decks; the Royal Hawaiian Band or other local musicians playing traditional Hawaiian music; dancers in ti leaf skirts performing the hula; cannons shooting streamers into the air; and stevedores clad in beautiful aloha shirts. On most occasions, volunteers greet disembarking passengers with fresh flower lei that say, "Aloha! Welcome to Oʻahu!"

Address: Aloha Boat Days
c/o Hawaiʻi Maritime Center
Pier 7, Honolulu Harbor
Honolulu, Hawaiʻi 96813
Phone: 523-6151
Web site: www.alohaboatdays.com

Volunteers greet passengers with lei and kisses.

◼ WAIMEA TOWN CELEBRATION

Sugar plantations have all but disappeared in Hawai'i, but fortunately a few community celebrations are still around that capture the flavor of that colorful era.

One of these is the Waimea Town Celebration sponsored by the West Kaua'i Main Street organization each February. Called the "biggest small-town party in Hawai'i," it showcases local crafts, products, music and sports in a town that was once the capital of Kaua'i, but is now located as far as possible from the island's political and business centers. That is the charm of this homegrown party, which is put on by a dedicated, enthusiastic cadre of volunteers. Continuous Hawaiian entertainment is onstage, while a variety of food favorites can be purchased to support local clubs, sports and youth organizations. Games and crafts round out the celebration.

Events are selected to appeal to residents but, as the West Kaua'i Main Street organizers say, "Visitors are welcome and treasured as guests." One highlight is the Paniolo Challenge, which features cowboys competing in relays, roping and mule racing.

The Plantation Days Film Festival takes place at the 500-seat Waimea Theater, a 1938 art deco picture palace that was restored in 1999. The Captain Cook Caper Fun Runs (two-, five- and ten-kilometer races); the Kilo-

Events like the Waimea Town Celebration foster community spirit. Photo by Chris Faye.

hana Long-Distance Canoe Race; a slow-pitch softball tournament; an 'ukulele contest; and an ice-cream-eating contest sponsored by Lappert's, which has been making ice cream on Kaua'i since 1983, are the main events offered.

On this trip down memory lane, however, don't think for a minute that Waimea is completely stuck in the past. The Paniolo Days Hat Lei Contest usually takes place at the West Kaua'i Technology and Visitor Center, which houses offices of high-tech businesses as well as companies serving the nearby Pacific Missile Range Facility.

Address: West Kaua'i Main Street
P.O. Box 903
Waimea, Hawai'i 96796
Phone: 335-2824
Web site: www.waimea.hawaiian.net/mainstreet/
waimeaprofile.html

■ MERRIE MONARCH FESTIVAL

Hilo is usually a sleepy old town, but once a year in April, every one of its hotel rooms is booked, rental cars are all taken and airline flights are sold out. This is the week of the Merrie Monarch Festival, Hawai'i's premier hula competition. It's been dubbed the "Olympics of hula" for the high caliber of performers who compete.

The Merrie Monarch Festival started in 1963 as an attempt to draw visitors to the lush east side of the Big Island. It floundered for a few years, but started to take off in 1971, when a hula contest was added to its usual lineup of arts and crafts demonstrations, historical exhibits and a parade.

The festival really boomed after 1976, when performances by male dancers were added and the competition stretched to three days. Hālau (hula schools) now vie for top recognition in eight categories, including Miss

Hālau Nā Mamo Pu'uanahulu performs in the ancient hula competition of the Merrie Monarch Festival.

Aloha Hula, where individual female dancers display their expertise in chanting, Hawaiian language, and kahiko (ancient) and 'auana (modern) hula.

The festival is named after King Kalākaua, nicknamed the Merrie Monarch. Kalākaua is credited with reviving many of the ancient Hawaiian songs, dances and chants that had been submerged when the New England missionaries arrived in 1820.

In many ways, though, the festival should be named after Dorothy "Aunty Dottie" Thompson, its unpaid octogenarian director. Aunty Dottie has run the festival almost from the beginning, and rules with an "iron hand." She is committed to keep the festival uncommercialized and true to its Hawaiian roots.

Some two dozen of the best hula hālau around the state and occasionally California spend much of the year raising money, designing costumes and perfecting dances for their appearance at Hilo's Edith Kanakaole Multi-Purpose Stadium. If you want to experience the thrill and drama of the Merrie Monarch Festival's hula competition, plan early. Tickets go on sale in January and often sell out within a month. Most people in Hawai'i watch the performances live on television or on the Internet at www.hawaiianchannel.com.

Address: Merrie Monarch Festival
c/o Hawai'i Naniloa Resort
93 Banyan Drive
Hilo, Hawai'i 96720
Phone: 935-9168

⊞ IN CELEBRATION OF CANOES

You could call this festival the "Great Canoe Carve-Off," but it's so much more. Every May, master carvers from Tonga, Tahiti, the Cook Islands, New Zealand and Hawai'i gather in historic Lahaina, the ancient capital of the Hawaiian kingdom, to carve traditional canoes from solid logs. Canoes brought the peoples of Polynesia to islands across the vast Pacific, and now they bring the people of Polynesia together to reassert a sense of cultural pride.

During Lahaina's festival of canoes, carvers share their traditional skills with the public, compare notes on both old-style hand adzes and modern power tools for creating their canoes, celebrate their united heritage in 'awa (kava) ceremonies and rejoice in the birthing of their creations as the canoes are launched into the sea for the first time. Over 20,000 people attend various events throughout the two-week celebration, most of which are free.

Canoe makers from different South Pacific islands demonstrate their craft.

The finished canoes are lined up on the beach, ready to be launched.

LahainaTown Action Committee organizes the festivities, which include a Parade of Canoes—both Maui County Canoe Racing outrigger canoes and the hand-carved canoes—down Lahaina's seaside Front Street. As the sun sets over the neighboring island of Lāna'i, top Hawai'i entertainers and warrior groups from the participating nations perform at the parade's ending point next to Lahaina Harbor.

As part of the festival's grand finale, the completed canoes are launched at the oceanfront Kamehameha Iki Park on Front Street, followed by the Festival of Canoes ho'olaule'a (celebration).

Address: LahainaTown Action Committee
648 Wharf Street
Lahaina, Hawai'i 96761
Phone: 667-9175
Web site: www.visitlahaina.com

KING KAMEHAMEHA CELEBRATION

No one knows exactly when Kamehameha the Great was born, although scholars say it was probably in November between 1748 and 1761 in North Kohala on the Big Island. After he unified the islands in 1810, Kamehameha I ruled in peace and established trade with foreign countries. He is sometimes called the "Napoleon of the Pacific."

By royal proclamation, Kamehameha's grandson, King Kamehameha V (Lot Kamehameha), designated June 11 of each year to honor Hawai'i's greatest statesman, warrior and monarch. The first commemoration, held on June 11, 1872, featured horse races, sack races, wheelbarrow and foot races. In 1901, a group of Hawaiian kūpuna (elders) first used flower lei to decorate the statue of Kamehameha that had been erected in Honolulu in 1883.

Draping this statue (as well as the two Kamehameha statues on the Big Island) with twenty-six-foot lei has since become a King Kamehameha Celebration tradition. Lei-draping ceremonies usually take place on the Friday nearest June 11.

In addition, the holiday is observed with floral parades on all the islands. Groups of beautifully coiffed equestriennes in flowing pā'ū, or long skirts, are definitely spectator favorites. You can tell which island a particular pā'ū unit is representing by the colors and blossoms the riders and horses are wearing. Each island has its own official color and flower.

King Kamehameha Celebration parades are scheduled on the Saturday nearest June 11, often ending with a folk life festival. A hula competition in Kamehameha's honor follows on O'ahu within two weeks.

The King Kamehameha Celebration Commission was established in 1939 to spearhead plans for the annual event. In 1998, Hawaiian Airlines and Grueninger Tours became the festival's leading sponsors when it seemed the fete would be cancelled because of lack of funding. The airline and tour company thus have kept alive the only holiday in the United States that was created to honor a once-reigning monarch in the only state that was once a kingdom.

**Address: King Kamehameha
Celebration Commission
355 North King Street
Honolulu, Hawai'i 96813
Phone: 586-0333
Web site: www.state.hi.us/dags/kkcc**

During the King Kamehameha Celebration, the statue of the mighty warrior and monarch in Honolulu is draped with flower lei.

PRINCE LOT HULA FESTIVAL
MOANALUA GARDENS

Prince Lot Kapu'aiwa, who ruled as King Kamehameha V from 1863 to 1872, is remembered for his energy, perseverance and strength of will. In the face of criticism from the Western community, he promoted the preservation of

The Prince Lot Hula Festival is Hawai'i's largest non-competitive hula event.

the Hawaiian culture. He sponsored traditional events, including hula performances, at his residence in the Moanalua district of O'ahu.

The Prince Lot Hula Festival, established in 1978 by the nonprofit Moanalua Gardens Foundation, is the largest and oldest non-competitive major hula event in Hawai'i. Every year since 1978, on the third Saturday in July, a dozen hālau (schools) from throughout the state perform ancient and modern hula. They dance on a dedicated earthen hula mound in the shade of the magnificent towering monkeypod trees of Moanalua Gardens, where Prince Lot's cottage is located.

Thousands of people attend the daylong event each year. The festival's permanent theme is Laukanaka Ka Hula, which means "a multitude of po'e hula (hula people) gather." It sums up the special feeling of this free event, which is a true celebration of the Hawaiian culture.

In addition to the hula performances, numerous demonstrations and exhibits fill Moanalua Gardens and its historic Chinese Hall, including lau hala (pandanus leaf) weaving; an art exhibit featuring the work of local artists; and traditional Hawaiian games, crafts and food.

Address: Moanalua Gardens Foundation
1352 Pineapple Place
Honolulu, Hawai'i 96819
Phone: 839-5334
Web site: mgf-hawaii.com

Performances by the keiki (children) are always crowd pleasers.

■ NA KA MAHINA
MĀLAMALAMA FESTIVAL
POLYNESIAN CULTURAL CENTER

One of Oʻahu's better-kept secrets is the Na Ka Mahina Mālamalama Festival, put on by the Polynesian Cultural Center in Lāʻie every August. The highlight of this daylong event, which honors the music, dance and culture of Hawaiʻi, is the Moanikeala Keiki ʻAuana Hula Competition. Moanikeala translates as "fragrant breeze;" keiki ʻauana means modern dances performed by children.

The festival pays tribute to two teachers who nurtured the growth of keiki hula in the Lāʻie community. Sally Wood Naluai, the Cultural Center's first hula instructor, began teaching youngsters in 1963 and oversaw the growth of the program for two decades. When

Pounding cooked taro root into poi.

she retired in 1981, she convinced her niece, Sunday Mariteragi—who once was a dancer at the Cultural Center herself—to follow in her footsteps.

The Na Ka Mahina Mālamalama Festival starts at 9:30 A.M. with a performance by as many as a dozen hālau (schools) that lasts until midday. It's a special thrill for participants and spectators alike, for the competition takes place in the breathtaking 2,775-seat Pacific Theater, a covered pavilion with a lush, tropical backdrop. This is where the Cultural Center's acclaimed Polynesian show takes place every evening but Sunday when the Center is closed.

The day continues with demonstrations and displays in the Hawaiian village. The event closes in the evening with entertainment by Hawaiian artists. Even better, you can enjoy reduced admission prices to the Polynesian Cultural Center on festival day.

**Address: 55-370 Kamehameha Highway
Lāʻie, Hawaiʻi 96762
Phone: 293-3333
Web site: www.polynesia.com**

You're never too young (or too old)
to do the hula!

■ FRANK B. SHANER HAWAIIAN FALSETTO CONTEST
HAWAII THEATRE CENTER

Hawaiian falsetto singing fits in a musical tradition that dates from the ancient chanters to the countertenors of the first Christian churches in the Islands to the yodeling of the paniolo (cowboys).

The singing is sweet and clear, with a gentleness that is all the more amazing when you consider the size of some of the men who sing it. Originally called leo wāhine (the women's voice), it is now known as leo ki'eki'e (high voice).

The first Frank B. Shaner Hawaiian Falsetto Contest was held at The Royal Hawaiian hotel's Monarch Room on O'ahu in 1995, with the Big Island's Clyde "Kindy" Sproat Falsetto and Storytelling Contest serving as its inspiration. Shaner—who is haole (Caucasian), Hawaiian, Portuguese and Chinese—is a stand-up comedian and one of Hawai'i's best-loved radio per-

A high, sweet falsetto can be rendered by even the biggest, most masculine of men.

sonalities. His contest caught on and has grown each year to become one of Aloha Festivals' largest fund-raising events.

Now presented in August in the beautiful Hawaii Theatre in downtown Honolulu, the event draws contestants from Japan and the Mainland as well as throughout Hawai'i. It helps preserve the art of falsetto and is simply a lot of fun. Among other prizes, winners record a CD courtesy of Hula Records, enabling them to reach a wider audience.

In addition to amateur contestants, the concert also spotlights some of Hawai'i's top musical stars.

Address: Aloha Festivals
Ward Warehouse
1060 Ala Moana Boulevard
Honolulu, Hawai'i 96814
Phone: 589-1771
Web site: www.alohafestivals.com

Frank B. Shaner (left) is in the spotlight with one of the winners of his Hawaiian Falsetto Contest.

■ ■ ■ ■ ■ ■ ALOHA FESTIVALS

Tourism officials refer to September and October as the "shoulder season," that time between visitors' summer vacations and their winter getaways.

Aloha Festivals aims to entice more visitors to the Islands during this time. Originally called Aloha Week, it started in 1946 when a group of former Jaycees decided to create a public celebration to honor Hawai'i's cosmopolitan heritage and preserve its music, dance and history.

Since then, the little event designed to showcase Hawaiian culture has grown to include hundreds of events on six islands spanning a two-month period, from late August to well into October. In 1991, to reflect its growth, Aloha Week became known as Aloha Festivals. Today, some visitors plan their vacations around Aloha Festivals events.

Each year, a new volunteer president heads the statewide celebration and selects the theme around which all events will revolve. Recent themes have included Hoʻohanohano I Nā Holokai (Honor the Voyagers), He Makana O Nā Lei Nani (A Gift of Beautiful Lei), Hui Pū I Ka Hula (Together in Song and Dance) and Ola Ka ʻOiwi (The Natives Endure).

Men and women of Hawaiian ancestry are recruited to make ceremonial appearances as their home island's Royal Court. For some appearances, they wear traditional Hawaiian attire; other times, they are dressed in the costumes of European royalty.

The Aloha Festivals Floral Parade on Oʻahu is ranked among the top three such parades in the nation. It is televised in Hawaiʻi in September, and then aired again nationwide as part of CBS network's Thanksgiving Day Special. Hotels, large retailers and other organizations create elaborate floats that require weeks of work by hundreds of volunteers. The results are truly phenomenal.

The Royal Ball and two massive hoʻolauleʻa (block parties) in downtown Honolulu and Waikīkī are other festival highlights, but

Floats, marching bands, equestrian units and more make the Floral Parade one of Aloha Festivals' most popular events. Photo by Bob Abraham.

they represent just the tip of the iceberg. Be sure to pick up an Aloha Festivals brochure and a $5 ribbon, which is your admission ticket to most events.

Address: P.O. Box 15945
Honolulu, Hawaiʻi 96830
Phone: 589-1771
Web site: www.alohafestivals.com

■ HĀPUNA BEACH PRINCE HOTEL SAM CHOY POKE FESTIVAL

The signature event of the Big Island's annual Aloha Festivals celebration, the Hāpuna Beach Prince Hotel Sam Choy Poke Festival, celebrates a popular local fish dish with a recipe contest, auction, banquet, concert and golf tournament. It's held the third weekend in September at Hāpuna Beach Prince Hotel on the Big Island's Kohala Coast and benefits the nearby Kawaihae Transitional Housing program, which assists homeless families and individuals.

Sam Choy is the one of the most Hawaiian of the new-wave chefs who introduced Hawai'i Regional Cuisine, which showcases locally grown produce, fish and meat. Poke is a mixture of raw fish, seaweed, onions and seasonings that's a staple at local lū'au.

The contest encourages both professional chefs and amateurs to enter their best poke dishes.

Entries include fun presentations as well as creative combinations of ingredients.

To be eligible for the poke contest, entries must include seafood from Hawaiian waters. There are ten categories, including traditional poke, cooked poke and poke using other ingredients, from tofu to macadamia nuts. For one category, only foods that existed in Hawai'i before Captain Cook arrived may be used.

The competition, which celebrated its tenth anniversary in 2001, is open to both professional chefs and novices; past winners include homemakers, a truck driver and a surfing instructor. Exhibiting the Islands' incredible diversity, recipes from past contests include Kim Chee Poke with Japanese Cucumber and Napa Cabbage, Poke Pizza, Volcano Tofu Poke, Poke Tempura and Spicy Mango Flavored Tako Poke with Tobiko Caviar.

Address: 62-100 Kauna'oa Drive
Kohala Coast, Hawai'i 96743
Phone: 880-3023
Web site: www.hapunabeachprincehotel.com

■ PRINCESS KAʻIULANI BIRTHDAY COMMEMORATION
SHERATON PRINCESS KAʻIULANI HOTEL

The story of Kaʻiulani—Hawaiʻi's fragile, hauntingly beautiful hapa-haole (half Hawaiian, half Caucasian) princess—strikes a sad but sweet chord in anyone who knows Island history. The daughter of Princess Miriam Likelike and Scottish-born Governor Archibald Cleghorn, Victoria Kaʻiulani (1875-1899) was the only child born to the Kalākaua dynasty. She was loved and admired as a linguist, musician, artist, equestrienne and swimmer, and was an active supporter of many charities.

Every year, the Sheraton Princess Kaʻiulani Hotel—which stands at the former entrance to ʻĀinahau, Kaʻiulani's Waikīkī home—recalls her life with a weeklong celebration called Hana Hoʻohiwahiwa O Kaʻiulani, In Celebration and Honor of Kaʻiulani. The commemoration is scheduled around the princess' birthday, October 16, with Hawaiian music, arts and crafts, cultural activities and its annual Keiki Hula Festival.

Later in the week, fifth-graders from nearby Kaʻiulani Elementary School perform songs, skits and dances that celebrate not only the princess' birthday, but also the founding of their school in 1899. That evening, a traditional royal procession of people representing Hawaiian nobility in monarchy attire begins at the ʻĀinahau Lobby and ends at the hotel's poolside lava rock stage, where a young woman portraying Kaʻiulani performs a lovely seated hula.

Finally, on the Saturday of celebration week, the princess' birthday is marked by a daylong arts-and-crafts fair and a Keiki Hula Festival featuring ten hula hālau (schools).

Children's hula performances delight guests at the annual commemoration of Princess Kaʻiulani's birthday.

Address: 120 Kaʻiulani Avenue
Honolulu, Hawaiʻi 96815
Phone: 922-5811
Web site: www.sheraton-hawaii.com

■ ANNUAL HAWAIIANA FESTIVAL
HYATT REGENCY KAUA'I RESORT & SPA

Each year in October, the Hyatt Regency Kaua'i Resort & Spa presents its Annual Hawaiiana Festival. In 2000, E Ho'i Mai I Ka Piko, or Return to the Source, was chosen as the theme for the festival. Hotel employees spend six months preparing for the daylong program, which is free and open to the public.

Reenacting a typical day in ancient Hawai'i, the festival begins with a sunrise cleansing ceremony of purification, using the water of Keoneloa Bay. Hotel employees design their attire for the day, with fabrics dyed with mud from a nearby beach as well as with Kaua'i's famous red dirt, believed to carry good luck. Using bamboo stamps, they imprint the fabrics with patterns of their 'aumakua (family deities), a traditional process that takes a full week to complete.

Visitors admire artisans weaving hats from lau hala (pandanus leaves).

In ancient times, royalty walked around Kaua'i, passing from one district to another with considerable pomp and ceremony. For this event, Aloha Festivals' Royal Court on Kaua'i is greeted at the edge of the Hyatt Regency Kaua'i Resort & Spa and escorted around the grounds to the hotel's Grand Ballroom, where a ceremony featuring conch shell blowing and chanting is presented.

Throughout the day, employees of the resort share their expertise in a variety of areas, from Ni'ihau shell lei making to herbal medicine to canoe carving. It is hard to say who has more fun—the hotel's staff or the visitors.

Address: 1571 Po'ipū Road
Kōloa, Hawai'i 96756
Phone: 742-1234
Web site: www.kauai-hyatt.com

The arrival of Kaua'i's Aloha Festivals Royal Court starts the day's activities.

CHRISTMAS AT THE HILTON
HILTON HAWAIIAN VILLAGE
BEACH RESORT & SPA

Every year, more than 10,000 visitors spend Christmas at O'ahu's Hilton Hawaiian Village, which seems to adopt "Deck the Halls" as its holiday motto. Decorations—always lovely, always lavish—change from year to year, with old favorites sometimes returning. Here's how the resort embellished its grounds and public areas one recent Christmas.

Did you say trees? "The Twelve Days of Christmas," that popular Christmas ditty, could be retitled "The Twelve Trees of Christmas" at the Hilton Hawaiian Village. The main lobby gets the grandest tree, which is festooned with beautiful porcelain dolls representing Hawai'i's ethnic diversity. Blue-and-red globes representing other islands throughout Polynesia also adorn the tree.

In the lobby of the Tapa Tower, you'll find the Hawaiian Tree, displaying handcrafted ornaments by local artisans. Commanding attention in the Ali'i Tower is the First Lady Tree, exhibiting a life-size coconut doll dressed in an elegant gown. A tree decorated with Chinese-style ornaments such as fans and chopsticks stands in the Golden Dragon restaurant.

Brightening the Paradise Lounge is a Hula Tree, decorated with 'ulī'ulī (feather-topped gourd rattles) and other Island-style ornaments.

In the main lobby, look for the Wildlife Tree, which calls attention to all the exotic animals that live at the Hilton Hawaiian Village.

The Tropics Bar is adorned with an Abundance of the Sea Tree, displaying sand dollars, seashells and sea horses. Embellishing the Shell Bar's Music Tree are musical instruments and festive ribbons.

It's Christmas Polynesian style at the Hilton Hawaiian Village!

A daily schedule of holiday concerts presented in the lobby is posted in the resort's public areas starting in early December. From children's choirs to big-name Island entertainers, the inspiring music is a good way to get in the holiday spirit.

Address: 2005 Kālia Road
Honolulu, Hawai'i 96815
Phone: 949-4321
Web site: www.hawaiianvillage.hilton.com

■ NEW YEAR'S AT THE SHERATON
SHERATON WAIKĪKĪ HOTEL

Sheraton is devoted to stamping out the rumor that there is no more Hawaiian music in Waikīkī, and the Sheraton Waikīkī is leading the crusade with its annual New Year's Show. Called Ho'omaka Hou (New Beginning), this musical extravaganza in the hotel's huge Hawai'i Ballroom features traditional and contemporary Island music and dance, in a choice of cocktail or dinner packages. There is even a kids' package with a special menu.

The evening starts at 6:00 P.M. New Year's Eve and ends after midnight, meaning you'll enjoy six hours of fabulous, nonstop Hawaiian entertainment. It's usually hosted by leading Island radio personalities who know how to keep a party hopping.

The show is always top-notch, boasting a mix of big-name stars, up-and-comers, and winners of various song and hula contests. There's even a Chinese lion dance to ward away evil spirits and help start the New Year

The Sheraton Waikīkī's New Year's show features top Hawaiian entertainment.

right. Reserve your tickets early; the event has been a sell-out in recent years.

Address: 2255 Kalākaua Avenue
Honolulu, Hawai'i 96815
Phone: 922-4422
Web site: www.sheratonhawaii.com

A distinctive surfboard marker calls attention to places
of interest on the Waikīkī Historic Trail.

The Nā Lehua Helelei images are dedicated
at Fort DeRussy in Waikīkī.

Honolulu is a great town for walking. Downtown, Chinatown and the Civic District are all close by and can be explored in a day or three days, as you choose.

You can find brochures for self-guided tours in the Governor's Office of Information at the State Capitol (Room 417; 586-0222) and at the King Kamehameha V Judiciary History Center on the first floor of Ali'iolani Hale (417 South King Street; 539-4999).

Some reasonably priced guided walking tours are offered as well. Call the Mission Houses Museum (531-0481), the Chinese Chamber of Commerce (533-3181) and Honolulu TimeWalks (943-0371) to inquire about their schedule of offerings.

Waikīkī is another walker's paradise. The Waikīkī Historic Trail, which you will read about on the next page, leads you to all the historical highlights of the area.

Hawai'i is far from famous for its monuments and markers, but there are more here than you might think. If you keep your eyes peeled around town, you can find Mahatma Gandhi (1869-1948); Jose Rizal, the Philippine author and patriot (1861-1896); and Dr. Sun Yat-sen (1866-1925), the first president of the Republic of China. Sun came to Hawai'i in the 1880s as a student and returned in the 1910s to raise money for the revolution in China.

But this chapter focuses on monuments that keep Hawai'i's past alive. Several of these stand in and around Waikīkī, and there are a few on the Big Island as well. Most of them have plaques to explain their historical significance. The Waikīkī Historic Trail markers are easy to read; they're as short and sweet as a history lesson can get. But watch for the pigeons.

■ WAIKĪKĪ HISTORIC TRAIL

There may never be a statue of the late Dr. George Kanahele, but many, many markers pay homage to him. Kanahele, who wrote the book *Restoring Hawaiianness to Waikīkī*, was the visionary champion of the Waikīkī Historic Trail, whose dozens of stops, indicated by surf-board-shaped markers, make this urban Polynesian resort a meaningful experience for all who visit.

Charles Palumbo, an architect from Lāna'i, designed the markers, which stand some six feet tall. Made of bronze and porcelain enamel, each cost $12,500. The markers are reminders that Waikīkī was a playground and seat of government for Hawaiian chiefs for centuries. Before it was drained, filled with coral and reconstructed mostly of concrete and steel, it also was home to thousands of Hawaiians, who lived and worked among its taro fields and fishponds.

You can follow the Waikīkī Historic Trail from any point, though it officially begins near the beach opposite the Honolulu Zoo and winds in the 'Ewa or westward direction to the Waikīkī Gateway Park with its King Kalākaua Statue.

Dr. Kanahele wrote the text that appears on the markers, in a booklet and on a Web site (a gift from LavaNet, an O'ahu-based Internet service provider), where you can take a virtual tour of the destination or download the trail brochure. Guided tours of the Waikīkī Historic Trail are available daily except Sunday. The Native Hawaiian Hospitality Association (founded by Kanahele) has established the program with support from the City and County of Honolulu and the Hawai'i Tourism Authority. The native Hawaiian guides sing, chant and share the history of Waikīkī along with personal family stories in an enthralling ninety-minute walk.

Beyond the trail—in the hotels, restaurants, shops and attractions of Hawai'i—there is a less tangible but just as real memorial to Kanahele. That is the hospitality and pride in Hawaiian culture that he taught to thousands who work in the visitor industry. That spirit of aloha is extended every day in countless ways to countless visitors.

Address: Native Hawaiian Hospitality Association
P.O. Box 295
Lā'ie, Hawai'i 96762
Phone: 841-6442
Web site: www.waikikihistorictrail.com

Joe Recca (left) and Patricia Lei Anderson Murray lead tours of the Waikīkī Historic Trail.

■ NĀ LEHUA HELELEI - FORT DERUSSY

Hawai'i has always revered its warriors, from the loyal soldiers of the ancient chiefs to young men and women who serve in the U.S. military today.

Those two traditions are melded in Nā Lehua Helelei, "the scattered lehua blossoms," a monument in front of the U.S. Army Museum at Randolph Battery near Waikīkī Beach at Fort DeRussy on O'ahu. The work was a labor of the heart by one of Hawai'i's most respected artists, Rocky Ka'iouliokahihikolo'ehu Jensen, leader of Hale Nauā III, Society of Hawaiian Arts.

When it was dedicated in 1999, the monument had been more than twenty years in Jensen's imagination. Back then, Thomas M. Fairfull, then director of the Army Museum, approached him with an idea for a simple plaque. That led to Jensen's notion of an image of Kū, the male principle and God of Summer, the season of war, then to five separate images, each nine feet tall, to represent five benign and healing aspects of Kū: The Beneficent, The Forgiver, The Life-Giver, The Benefactor and The Steadfast.

Members of the Order of Kamehameha present offerings at the dedication of Nā Lehua Helelei. Photo by Thomas Fairfull of the Army Museum.

Jensen supported the project through grants and the generosity of others, including the donation of the 'ōhi'a logs used to make the images. With the help of the Office of Hawaiian Affairs and the Hawai'i Community Foundation, the project also became an apprenticeship program, teaching sculpting to a new generation of artists.

The result is believed to be the largest Hawaiian carving endeavor since Kamehameha the Great ordered the refurbishing of Hawai'i's heiau (places of worship) in 1810. It is well worth a trip to Waikīkī to see the images, which have been described as the best of Hawai'i's outdoor art. Nā Lehua Helelei stands as a tribute to native Hawaiian art, a gift to the courage and undaunted spirit of native Hawaiian warriors, past and present.

Address: U.S. Army Museum
2055 Kālia Road
Honolulu, Hawai'i 96815
Phone: 438-2819

Ancient kane (male) hula adds drama to the dedication ceremony. Photo by Thomas Fairfull of the Army Museum.

▪ ▪ ▪ KAMEHAMEHA THE GREAT

Four massive bronze statues honor the great warrior King Kamehameha, and they have four interesting stories. In 1878, King Kalākaua commissioned a statue of King Kamehameha I for $10,000. An American artist in Italy sculpted the nine-ton statue, and after it was bronzed in Paris, it was shipped to Hawai'i. Caught in a huge storm, the ship sank off the Falkland Islands, and the statue was lost.

Although it was recovered, the original statue was delivered in March 1882 in badly damaged condition with an arm missing. With the insurance money, a replica was ordered, which arrived January 31, 1883 aboard the *Aberman*. That ship also brought along a replacement arm for the original. The replica was placed in front of Ali'iolani Hale, the Judiciary Building in downtown Honolulu on O'ahu. The original was repaired and erected where it now stands in Kapa'au town, in the North Kohala district of the Big Island, near Kamehameha's birthplace.

When Hawai'i became a state in 1959, it was entitled to install two statues in Statuary Hall in the U.S. Capitol. The State Legislature approved statues of Father Damien and King Kamehameha. Weighing nine tons and standing eight-and-a-half feet high, the statue of Kamehameha is the largest statue to be displayed at the Capitol. The unveiling on April 15, 1969 was accompanied by the blowing of a conch shell, a chanter, kāhili (royal feather standard) bearers and the presentation of lei. In 1997, a fourth and different Kamehameha statue was erected at Wailoa State Park in Hilo on the Big Island. It had been commissioned by the Princeville Corporation for its luxurious resort on Kaua'i, but Kaua'i's Hawaiian community objected, since theirs was the one island Kamehameha had not conquered. They didn't want the statue.

So it stayed in storage until it was gifted to the Kamehameha Schools Alumni Association-East Hawai'i, who raised the funds to ship it to Hilo, where it was erected on June 10, 1997. Measuring fourteen feet (eighteen feet if you count the spear), the Hilo statue is the tallest image of Kamehameha ever created. But the Honolulu statue is still the most famous and most photographed. The Friday before the King Kamehameha Celebration parade, the statue is draped with twenty-six-foot-long garlands of fresh flowers.

An imposing statue of King Kamehameha stands in front of Ali'iolani Hale in downtown Honolulu.
Photo by Ann Cecil.

■ ■ KING KALĀKAUA

Two statues honor David La'amea Kalākaua, a high chief who was elected the seventh king of Hawai'i in 1874. Kalākaua was nicknamed the Merrie Monarch for his love of a good party and his devotion to reviving the ancient hula and chants that had been submerged in deference to the beliefs of the Christian missionaries.

Robert Louis Stevenson described Kalākaua as a "fine and intelligent man." A gifted musician and author, the king wrote Hawai'i's national anthem, now the State Song, *Hawai'i Pono'ī*, and the book *The Legends and Myths of Hawai'i*, which is still in print.

Kalākaua was the first monarch to travel around the world. He commissioned the building of 'Iolani Palace and had electricity installed there in 1887, before Buckingham Palace and the White House.

In Hilo on the Big Island, his statue is in Kalākaua Park, surrounded by huge banyan trees. Here, the king is seated, holding an ipu heke (double gourd hula instrument) in one hand and a taro plant, from which the Hawaiian staple poi is made, in the other. These symbolize Kalākaua's commitment to nurture his people.

In O'ahu's Waikīkī Gateway Park, where Kūhiō Avenue and Kalākaua Avenue split, is another King Kalākaua statue. This one was commissioned in 1985, when O'ahu observed the Kanyaku Imin Centennial, the 100th

This statue in Waikīkī honors Kalākaua, Hawai'i's last reigning king. Photo by Ann Cecil.

anniversary of the arrival of the first Japanese contract laborers brought to Hawai'i to work on the plantations. It was erected in 1991.

Kalākaua had visited Japan in 1881 and signed a labor import agreement. In all, 220,000 Japanese immigrants came to the Islands from 1885 to 1924. Today, many of their descendants are the leaders of Hawai'i.

Amid growing political turmoil between native Hawaiians and foreign businessmen, Kalākaua died in 1891 while visiting San Francisco. His sister, Lili'uokalani, ascended the throne but within two years, the monarchy was overthrown. The Kalākaua Statue is a stop on the Waikīkī Historic Trail.

■ QUEEN LYDIA LILI'UOKALANI

Outside the State Capitol, a statue of Queen Lili'uokalani, Hawai'i's last reigning monarch, stands on the mall facing 'Iolani Palace. She became queen in 1891, upon the death of her brother King Kalākaua. When she attempted to restore the power of the monarchy and preserve the rights of the native Hawaiian people, she was deposed by foreign businessmen and others who favored Hawai'i's annexation by the United States.

With a militia backed by marines from an American ship in Honolulu Harbor, they formed a provisional government and took control. In 1898, after five years as a republic, Hawai'i was annexed to the United States.

Lili'uokalani was married to an American, John Dominis Holt, but he died shortly after she became queen. They lived in his family home, called Washington Place, located across from the State Capitol. Washington Place has been the home of Hawai'i's governors since before statehood.

In 1895, Hawaiians loyal to Lili'uokalani staged a revolt that was crushed. She was arrested and lived under detention in an upper room of 'Iolani Palace for eight months. At the start of World War I, Lili'uokalani raised the Stars and Stripes over Washington Place for the first time, in a show of solidarity with the young Hawaiian men serving with the U.S. military forces. She died in 1917.

The Queen Lili'uokalani statue was dedicated in April 1982. She holds a copy of "Aloha 'Oe," the best known of the many songs she wrote; the Constitution she tried to promulgate before she was overthrown; and the *Kumulipo,* the creation chant that chronicles the ancient genealogy of the Hawaiian people.

Queen Lili'uokalani was deposed in 1893, setting the stage for Hawai'i to be annexed by the United States. Photo by Ann Cecil.

■ PRINCESS KA'IULANI STATUE

Princess Victoria Ka'iulani, who died at the tender age of twenty-three in 1899, is an especially beloved and tragic figure in Hawaiian history. As the only child born to the Kalākaua dynasty, she was groomed for the throne.

Many places honor her memory, but the newest, located on O'ahu, may be one of the best. In a park at the corner of Kūhiō and Ka'iulani avenues in Waikīkī, across from the Outrigger East Hotel, stands a new statue of the princess, a donation by the entrepreneurial Kelley family and their Outrigger hotels and resorts, many of which are located nearby.

As part of making a gift of the statue to the people of Hawai'i, the Kelley family and Outrigger "adopted" the small park from the City and County of Honolulu and renovated it. This is the last bit of open space left from Ka'iulani's twelve-acre family estate, 'Āinahau, "land of the hau trees."

The Kelley family commissioned sculptor Jan Gordon Fisher to create the eight-foot work of art that weighs 800 pounds. The princess wears a Victorian dress with a peacock (pīkake in Hawaiian) at her feet. She was affectionately called the "Peacock Princess" for the flocks of the beautiful birds that roamed her estate. She wears a three-strand lei of Chinese jasmine (also

Princess Ka'iulani is immortalized in bronze with one of her beloved peacocks.

called pīkake in Hawaiian), her favorite flower.

Unveiled in 1999 on the 124th anniversary of the princess' birth, the statue also bears a plaque detailing her royal bloodline and major events in her life. It is part of the Waikīkī Historic Trail that weaves through the seaside resort area.

■ DUKE KAHANAMOKU STATUE

To millions around the world, Duke Kahanamoku symbolized Hawai'i. A full-blooded Hawaiian, he was born in Waikīkī in 1890, and spent many hours as a boy and youth playing in the warm Pacific. He proved his prowess in water sports, and many knew he would one day be a champion swimmer.

Between 1912 and 1932, Kahanamoku won three gold medals, two silver and four bronze in four Olympics. He is known as the father of international surfing for introducing the sport of Hawaiian kings to Australia, Europe and the U.S. East Coast.

Kahanamoku worked as a movie actor in Hollywood for many years, and from 1934 to 1960, he served as sheriff of Honolulu for thirteen consecutive terms. Until his death in 1968, he was considered the unofficial mayor of Waikīkī and Hawai'i's ambassador of aloha.

A true hero, Kahanamoku saved eight people from a capsized launch at Corona Del Mar, California in 1925, using his surfboard. When he died, thousands lined Waikīkī Beach to see his ashes scattered in the ocean beyond the reef by the Rev. Abraham Akaka of Kawaiaha'o Church.

Kahanamoku was a person who was larger than life, and his larger-than-life statue stands before an old-fashioned surfboard on Waikīkī Beach on O'ahu. It caused quite a stir when it was first erected. Hawaiian watermen never turn their back on the ocean, you see, and surfers who idealized Kahanamoku said he would never turn his back on a wave.

Today, thousands of visitors have their picture taken in front of Kahanamoku's statue, and his outstretched arms are regularly draped with leis. This monument is the fifth stop on the Waikīkī Historic Trail.

The legendary Duke Kahanamoku still greets visitors to Waikīkī Beach.

Exploring the Ka'elekū Cavern at Hāna, Maui.

Hāhālua Lele skims the waves off the Kona Coast of the Big Island.

The Hawai'i Visitors & Convention Bureau calls Hawai'i the "Islands of Discovery." It is more than a mere slogan. There really are amazing things to discover here, some that you won't find anywhere else in the world.

The Hawaiian Islands are the most remote landmass on Earth. This means two things. First, everything that came here—fish, birds, plants, animals and, of course, people—did so over long distances at great cost in time and energy. Second, once they got here, they interacted, often undergoing changes as they adapted to their new environment.

The museums and tours in this chapter will help you learn about Hawai'i, in all its splendor, in all its uniqueness. It is far from an exhaustive list. But the places listed here have been part of the Hawai'i Visitors & Convention Bureau's Keep It Hawai'i Program, which means that great care has been taken to ensure authenticity and accessibility.

Hawaiian culture is so focused on hospitality, on "welcoming the stranger," that real pride is taken in sharing. No meal ever seems to reach a point where there is not enough food to invite one more person to eat. Local people, especially in the visitor industry, dole out hospitality in the same way. E komo mai! Welcome! There's always room for one more.

◼ GAY & ROBINSON
SUGAR PLANTATION TOUR

For generations, sugar was king in Hawai'i, and plantations dotted all the islands. Entire towns—complete with schools, houses, hospitals and churches—were built around the fields and mills. The plantation was in itself a separate community.

Today, the only place to tour a working plantation is at the remotest end of the remotest Hawaiian island. That's on the far west side of Kaua'i, where Gay & Robinson Company maintains its headquarters and 7,500 acres of cane. The United States' trade policies and foreign government subsidies have led to the decline of domestic sugar production over the past few decades, including that of Hawai'i. In fact, Gay & Robinson, a family-owned company, is one of the last two working plantations in the state. Still, it holds the distinction of being the highest-yielding plantation (in terms of tons of sugar produced per acre) in the world—a tribute to management, technology, dedicated workers, and the property's rich soil and climate.

Guides conduct the two-hour bus tour down private plantation roads and into the factory. Sugar processing is in full swing from April through October, so that is the best time to take the tour of the fields and factory. The product Gay & Robinson manufactures is brown, not white, since the final refining takes place in California.

Work on a sugar plantation is not sweet; it is hot and dirty. You should wear pants or shorts and low-heeled, closed-toe shoes; hard hats and goggles are provided. The tour is limited to twenty-five people, the number the bus can seat. No time for a tour? Feel free to stop at the company's visitor center to peruse its historic displays of plantation life.

Also available is a three-hour upland tour of Gay & Robinson sugar fields and ranch lands that offers spectacular views of rugged Olokele Canyon where *Jurassic Park* and *George of the Jungle* were filmed. You will see Kaua'i the way many local people do—riding in a pickup truck.

Because it goes along unpaved back roads, the tour is contingent on weather. In case of heavy rain, you can opt to take a shorter tour, which doesn't traverse unpaved plantation roads.

Address: 2 Kaumakani Avenue
Kaumakani, Hawai'i 96747
Phone: 335-2824
Hours: The visitor center is open from 8:00 A.M. to 4:00 P.M. Monday through Friday; check-in for the tours is at 8:45 A.M. and 12:45 P.M.
Web site: www.gandrtours-kauai.com

Visitors examine newly planted sugarcane at Gay & Robinson's fields on Kaua'i's west end.
Photo by Kay Koike.

■ HĀHĀLUA LELE
THE ORCHID AT MAUNA LANI

Two things set a Hawaiian vacation apart: the experience of Hawai'i's unique culture and the chance to feel the aloha spirit up close and personal. Both benefits are available aboard the *Hāhālua Lele*, Flying Manta Ray, a thirty-five-foot double-hulled Hawaiian sailing canoe that sails from The Orchid at Mauna Lani on the Big Island.

Built with loving care and captained by Casey Cho, *Hāhālua Lele* is modeled after a famous Waikīkī surfing canoe, *Ka Mō'ī*, built in the 1930s. Cho used koa, ōhi'a and hau woods for the canoe's body, and patterned the main sail after the ancient Hawaiians' traditional crab claw design.

The traditional 'iako (outrigger boom) lashings were constructed by students of the Hawaiian Studies Program at Konawaena High School under the supervision of Clay Bertleman and the crew of *Makali'i*, one of *Hāhālua Lele's* larger, ocean-going canoe cousins. Unlike the bigger voyaging canoes— *Makali'i, Hōkūle'a* and *Hawai'i Loa*—*Hāhālua Lele* was not built for ocean crossings but for sailing along the Kohala Coast. The two-hour expedition is the perfect platform for Cho to teach novice sailors about the sea, Hawaiian folklore and customs, and the amazing naviga-

The *Hāhālua Lele*, a double-hulled Hawaiian sailing canoe, takes visitors on exhilarating tours.

tional skills of the ancient Polynesians. It is also a great way to see the Kona-Kohala Coast from the ocean, and find some great swimming and snorkeling spots.

A visitor from California summed up the *Hāhālua Lele* experience in the tour's guest book: "It is uplifting to spend a few hours with you and your crew on the canoe. It is a joy to see you keeping such an important and beautiful part of Hawai'i's culture alive."

**Address: One North Kanikū Drive
Kohala Coast, Hawai'i 96743
Hours: 8:00 and 11:00 A.M., 2:00 P.M. daily
except Sunday, weather permitting
Phone: 885-2000
Web site: www.orchid-maunalani.com**

▓ MAUI CAVE ADVENTURES

Maui Cave Adventures offers nature lovers a chance to explore the eighteenth-largest lava tube cave system in the world under the careful guidance of experienced caving guides. The lava tube is called Ka'elekū Caverns and the place is Hāna, one of the remotest and loveliest spots in Hawai'i. Ka'elekū means "stand in a dark hollow place." You will understand the name as you explore the 30,000-year-old cavern.

On the Scenic Walking Tour, for those aged eight and up, claustrophobia is no problem. The cave's cathedral-high ceilings are thirty to forty feet high, and a cool breeze blows through open-air skylights. You can see beautiful colors and inspect the diversity of formations left by an underground river of lava.

The Wild Adventure Tour continues into narrow crawl spaces, over rocky ledges and up a twenty-foot ladder where you can explore hidden chambers and hideaways. For this tour, participants must be at least fifteen years old and be physically fit.

Until 1970, the cave was used to dispose of bones from Hāna's slaughterhouse. Chuck Thorne, who operates Maui Cave Adventures, spent eight months single-handedly removing over 15,000 pounds of waste—one thirty-pound bucket at a time—to return the cavern to its natural beauty and make it fit to visit.

Guides teach hikers to touch nothing and cave softly. It's an excellent opportunity to learn about volcanoes and the geology of the Islands. Plan to wear long pants and close-toed shoes. Thoughtfully, Maui Cave Adventures supplies hard hats, flashlights and thick gloves that you probably would not pack for your average trip to Hawai'i.

Address: P.O. Box 40
Hāna, Hawai'i 96713
Phone: 248-7308
Hours: 11:00 A.M. and 1:00 P.M. daily
except Sunday
Web site: www.mauicave.com

Spelunkers take a break in a chamber of the Ka'elekū Caverns.

■ MAUKA MAKAI EXCURSIONS

Eco-tourism is a term that still confuses people. Dominic Kealoha Aki, president of Mauka Makai Excursions, recalls, "The 'eco' in eco-tourism stands for ecology, but I've had people call and ask if we were an economy tour. I tell them, 'No, but how much do you have? I'll work with you.'"

Aki established Mauka Makai Excursions in January 1998 to offer cultural, archaeological and hiking eco-tours to areas of O'ahu rarely seen by most visitors. It is one of a growing number of small, personalized tour companies whose mission is to educate participants about environmental conservation in addition to showing them a fun time.

For most visitors, trying to find unmarked spots that are seldom listed in tour guides would be daunting, perhaps dangerous. Mauka Makai's knowledgeable guides take

Mauka Makai Excursions, launched by Dominic Aki (right), takes O'ahu visitors off the beaten track. Photo by Tami Dawson.

Hawaiian history comes to life with the help of a good trail guide. Photo by Tami Dawson.

them off the beaten path to legendary places and sacred sites. A special appreciation of history and the environment comes when your guide takes the time, before going into a heiau or place of worship, to utter a prayer asking the spirits who dwell there for permission to enter.

Mauka Makai's half- and full-day treks for two to ten people vary in difficulty. Tour prices include insect repellent, bottled water, rain gear, backpacks and beach supplies. Upon request, Mauka Makai also can arrange day hikes to very remote spots that many local residents don't even know about, as well as special excursions like evening torch fishing.

Address: 350 Ward Avenue
Honolulu, Hawai'i 96814
Phone: 593-3525
Hours: Most tours begin with a
7:30 A.M. hotel pickup.
Web site: www.oahu-ecotours.com

■ MOLOKA'I MULE RIDE

Of the many spiritual, even mystical, experiences in Hawai'i, none compares to a pilgrimage to Kalaupapa, the settlement on Moloka'i where those suffering from Hansen's disease (leprosy) were banished in the mid-1800s. The Hawaiian government began exiling those unfortunate souls to this barren spit of land on the island's north coast in 1866. Rough seas and rugged 1,700-foot-high cliffs made this a lonely, desolate site indeed.

Adventurers make their way down the steep trail to Kalaupapa on the backs of surefooted mules. Photo courtesy of Maui Visitors Bureau.

With no shelter and few provisions, the colony was a lawless, godforsaken place until the Belgian priest Joseph Damien de Veuster arrived in 1873 to minister to the condemned. Father Damien eventually contracted Hansen's disease himself, and succumbed to it in 1889.

Today, Damien has been beatified and only about fifty elderly patients remain at Kalaupapa. Sulfone drugs arrested the disease in the mid-1940s. While the patients are free to travel, they feel more comfortable staying in the isolated settlement where they have lived most of their lives. Kalaupapa was designated a national historical park in 1980.

Of the three ways to get there—by air, foot or mule—by far the best is to go in (and therefore out) with the Moloka'i Mule Ride. The surefooted mules know the way down the steep, narrow 2.9-mile trail, which has twenty-six switchbacks. It's a harrowing experience at first, but once you trust your mount, you can concentrate on the incredible views that unfold at every turn.

At the bottom of the trail, a guide from Damien Tours—run by Richard Marks, the unofficial mayor of Kalaupapa—meets you. You'll visit Father Damien's grave site, St. Philomena Church, which he built, and more. Reservations are a must, since no one may visit Kalaupapa "uninvited." Also note that the national park is closed Sundays and that no children under the age of sixteen are admitted.

Address: P.O. Box 200
Kualapu'u, Hawai'i 96757
Phone: 567-6088
Hours: Seven-and-a-half-hour tour begins at
8:00 A.M. daily except Sunday
Web site: www.muleride.com

Experienced muleskinners are in charge of the Moloka'i Mule Ride. Photo courtesy of MVB/ Ron Dahlquist.

■ SENATOR FONG'S PLANTATION AND GARDENS

Hiram Fong represented Hawai'i in the U.S. Congress for seventeen years, starting with statehood in 1959. The son of Chinese immigrants, he was the first Asian-American ever elected to the U.S. Senate and had a long and successful career as a businessman and politician.

Today, the genial nonagenarian is still forging new paths—with a shovel and cane knife. Senator Fong's most enduring legacy—and by his own description, his greatest joy—is this garden, which covers a breathtaking 725 acres beneath the majestic Ko'olau Mountains overlooking Kāne'ohe Bay on O'ahu. Visitors often see the retired senator working tirelessly in the gardens, much of which he planted himself.

Fong started buying the land in 1950. For a time, he operated a banana plantation. Then in 1988, he opened Senator Fong's Plantation and Gardens, realizing a dream he had nurtured for much of his life.

Today, his gardens encompass plateaus of exotic fruit, hillsides of palms and ferns, and valleys of flowers. Many of the plants have

Many of the plants, like the ti shown in the foreground here, have great cultural significance to the people of Hawai'i. Photo by Chelsea Fong Calunod.

great cultural significance to the native Hawaiians and immigrant cultures that make up Hawai'i. Highlights include 100 fragrant sandalwood trees, a species that barely survived heavy barter with traders in the days of the Hawaiian monarchy; pili grass, once used to thatch houses and now a rarity on O'ahu; and over eighty varieties of palm, including the only endemic Hawaiian palm, the lo'ulu.

A narrated tram tour takes visitors through five plateaus and valleys named after presidents with whom Fong served in Washington: Eisenhower, Kennedy, Johnson, Nixon and Ford. Senator Fong hopes his gardens will be a lasting legacy—a haven where visitors, particularly future generations of Hawai'i's children, can come to enjoy the beauty of the plants and flowers, and learn about the significant roles they've played in the history and lifestyle of the Islands.

Address: 47-285 Pūlama Road
Kāne'ohe, Hawai'i 96744
Phone: 239-6775
Hours: 10:00 A.M. to 4:00 P.M. daily except
Christmas Day and New Year's Day
Web site: www.fonggarden.net

Hundreds of varieties of flowers and plants brighten Senator Fong's Plantation and Gardens. Photo by Chelsea Fong Calunod.

■ TEMPTATION TOURS

A trip to Hāna on Maui is a journey back in time and a real test if you choose go there by car; the famous Hāna Highway has over 600 hairpin curves and fifty-four one-lane bridges. It's actually fortunate that you're forced to drive slowly, so you won't miss the breathtaking scenery all along the way—white-crested waves battering ebony cliffs, waterfalls spilling into pools just a few feet from the road, fruit and flowers in exuberant abundance.

The challenge of getting to Hāna (and back) is half the experience. Once there, you'll be captivated by the town's rustic charm. It's no wonder many people call it "heaven on earth."

Owned and operated by Dave and Kathy Campbell since 1986, Temptation Tours offers three tours to Hāna, each limited to six or eight guests who are seated in a comfortable "Limo-Van." One tour includes a helicopter flight—an easy way to tackle the grueling road.

Among the stops are Kakala Gardens, a fifty-acre preserve of beautiful tropical flowers, and the Heritage Museum at Pā'ia Plantation. Views of the East Maui Irrigation Waterways offer participants a chance to learn about its amazing history.

Temptation Tours takes culture as seriously as comfort. Its guides are certified through Maui Community College's Visitor Industry Training and Economic Development Center. More training comes from Sam Ka'ai, a respected leader in the Native Hawaiian Hospitality Association.

Tour participants also receive the *Hana and Beyond* video, which means they can relax on the trip and enjoy the scenery through their eyes instead of the viewfinders of their camcorders. They can relive the entire experience when they pop the video into their VCRs at home.

Temptation Tours also offers four Haleakalā Crater tours that include (in various combinations) stops at the Pā'ia Plantation, Thompson Ranch in Kula, Tedeschi Vineyards, a protea farm, Kula Lodge and Makawao town—in short, the best that Upcountry Maui has to offer.

Address: 211 Ahinahina Place
Kula, Hawai'i 96790
Phone: 877-8888
Hours: Seven tours daily, beginning at 3:30,
7:00 and 11:15 A.M.
Web site: www.temptationtours.com

This is a stress-free way to make the scenic but long trip to Hāna, Maui.

■ WAIKĪKĪ TROLLEY

Mark Twain called Hawai'i "the loveliest fleet of islands anchored in any ocean," but if he were to return to Honolulu today, he would probably think, at least for a moment, that he had been transported to San Francisco. All around him he would see what look like San Francisco's famed cable cars, minus the cables. Trolleys have become a common sight on Honolulu's streets mainly because of the E Noa Corporation.

E Noa's Waikīkī Trolleys carry 45,000 passengers a month around O'ahu, many of them visitors. Well-trained drivers and guides make riding the trolley a fun educational experience. You can see the island's major sights, get on and off as you please, and customize your sightseeing without renting a car and enduring the stress of navigating through traffic.

The Waikīkī Trolleys cruise along five routes: the Red City Line explores historic Honolulu; the Yellow Shopping and Dining Line stops at O'ahu's popular malls and restaurants; the Blue Ocean Coast Line heads east as far as Sea Life Park; the Purple First Adventures Line includes Diamond Head Crater, the National Memorial Cemetery of the Pacific (Punchbowl) and the State Capitol; and the Orange Hidden Treasures Line goes to the Pali Lookout, Makapu'u Lookout and Hanauma Bay.

In all, the trolleys can take you to over two dozen popular spots on O'ahu. The Red Line is the only regular visitor transportation that directly serves the Bishop Museum. It stops there seventeen times a day, as part of the company's commitment to get visitors to institutions of cultural and educational interest on O'ahu, not just to places where they can play and shop.

All aboard E Noa's Waikīkī Trolley!

Address: 1141 Waimanu Street
Honolulu, Hawai'i 96814
Phone: 593-2822
Hours: Trolleys run from 8:27 A.M. to
11:48 P.M. daily
Web site: www.waikikitrolley.com

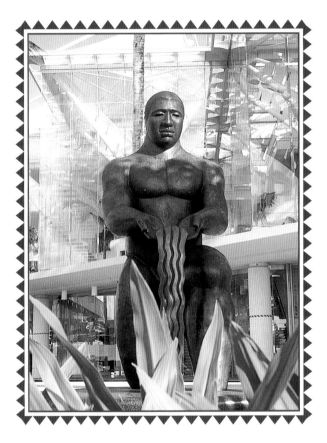

The *Gift of Water* by Shige Yamada welcomes
visitors to the Hawai'i Convention Center.

A collage of pretty faces and places adorns the back cover of
the book *Waikīkī, in the Wake of Dreams.*

O ver the decade that the Hawai'i Visitors & Convention Bureau has sponsored the Keep It Hawai'i program, the number of categories has grown to eighteen. No doubt there will be more.

Still, no matter how many categories are created, there are always entries that don't fit anywhere. What to do?

In keeping with the Hawaiian tradition of inclusiveness—there is always room for another guest at the table, after all—the Special Category was created.

When something comes along that doesn't fit in an existing category, that is pretty special, isn't it? (Of course, we believe every entry in this book is special in its own way.)

For example, the Hawai'i Convention Center is one of a kind. It is like no other facility in the state. Indeed, with its unique Hawaiian sense of place, it is like no other convention center anywhere on Earth. It would be unfair to judge it against anything else.

Similarly, Billy Fields is a mason who keeps alive a way of building stone walls and platforms that dates back to ancient times in Hawai'i. It is a construction technique that he perpetuates as much for the sake of tradition as for the sake of building. It would be difficult to compare his contributions with those of the lei weaver or the tapa maker.

This chapter spotlights unusual efforts some people and organizations are making to Keep It Hawai'i.

■ ▓ ■ ■ BILLY FIELDS MASONRY

As you stroll along Kalākaua Avenue in Waikīkī between the Sheraton Moana Surfrider Hotel and the Duke Kahanamoku Statue, pause to observe the Healing Stones of Kapeaemahu. Legend says they are a tribute to four healers with magical powers who came to Hawai'i from Tahiti before the sixteenth century. Before they vanished, they infused the stones with their power.

The nearest stones of this kind on O'ahu are found at least two miles away. How the Healing Stones, which weigh as much as eight tons each, got to the Waikīkī site when the Hawaiians had no wheeled vehicles or animals to pull them is a mystery.

Before the present platform and enclosure were built in 1997 under the sponsorship of the Queen Emma Foundation, the stones were treated with little respect—as towel racks or worse. Under the direction of the late "Papa" Henry Auwae, a traditional Hawaiian healer, a proper setting was constructed. The person who did that painstaking work was Billy Fields, a licensed mason who's a master of uhauhumu pōhaku, dry stack rock construction that uses no mortar. In this ancient Hawaiian method, a wall's stability relies on stones placed one atop another so they lock into place.

Fields studied centuries-old walls and talked to elderly masons to learn the technique. He has restored many structures throughout the state in this manner, including ancient places of worship, burial sites and fishponds. Tucked along back roads and in wilderness regions, many of these sites are difficult to find.

On the Big Island, however, two other examples of Fields' handiwork are easily accessible. He built the stone walls around Hulihe'e Palace on Ali'i Drive in Kailua-Kona town as well as the wall for a nearby fishpond. Although Fields used concrete mortar for these structures and for the enclosure that surrounds the Healing Stones of Kapeaemahu, they exhibit the same meticulous craftsmanship that marks walls he has constructed in the traditional Hawaiian way.

When Fields begins a restoration, he always studies the proper chants and rituals needed to enter a historic site. In 2001, as a recognized master of uhauhumu pōhaku, he was invited to attend the Smithsonian Institution Folk Life Festival on the Mall in Washington, D.C., which draws more than a million visitors each year.

Address: P.O. Box 924
Kailua-Kona, Hawai'i 96745
Phone: 325-6136

Billy Fields restored the walls of this agricultural heiau (place of worship) in Manō Valley on O'ahu.
Photo courtesy of Fields Masonry.

▦ HAWAI'I CONVENTION CENTER

When Hawai'i set out to build a Convention Center, all agreed that it should be like no other, a facility that would exude a "Hawaiian sense of place."

The result was an award-winning structure that architectural judges have described as "a living work of art," that can "uplift the human spirit through advanced technologies."

In short, it's worth taking a look around this building.

In addition to a superb design by Seattle-based LMN Architects and Wimberly Allison Tong & Goo—a Hawai'i firm known for resort architecture around the world—the Convention Center showcases more original artwork than any other building in Hawai'i. Its $2-million collection includes eye-catching pieces by local youth and a restored fresco by the late Jean Charlot.

Inside, paintings of volcanoes, mountains, ocean, waterfalls, taro and fishponds are displayed alongside images of Hawaiian royalty, gods and mythical creatures. Soaring rooftop canopies emulate the sails of ancient Polynesian canoes.

A three-story indoor waterfall and a 2.5-acre landscaped rooftop tropical garden set the $350-million building apart. So do the fiber optic cabling, multilingual translation stations and satellite video conferencing of its state-of-the-art telecommunications technology.

The Convention Center's grand opening celebration in June 1998 was a gala black-tie affair, with canoes arriving at the Ala Wai Canal's boat landing. Since then, a range of events—from the Miss Universe pageant coronation to conventions of professional groups such as the American Dental Association to international economic summits, including the Asian Development Bank—have filled its exhibit halls, theaters and conference rooms. While some functions are private, community events like the ten-day Hawai'i International Film Festival also are held at the Convention Center; call to check on events that may be open to the public.

Through its Ambassadors of Aloha Program, the Convention Center utilizes community volunteers to conduct tours. To schedule a tour, please call 943-3587.

Address: 1801 Kalākaua Avenue
Honolulu, Hawai'i 96815
Phone: 943-3500
Web site: www.hawaiiconvention.com

The Hawai'i Convention Center overlooks the Ala Wai Canal. Photo by Olivier Koning.

■ HO'OKIPA ALOHA COUNCIL

The next time you pass through Honolulu International Airport on O'ahu, look for the Ho'okipa Aloha Council. Ho'okipa means "hospitality,' and the organization's way of showing that is to make transiting the airport a unique experience of aloha.

Made up chiefly of volunteers, the Aloha Council supports a number of ongoing programs. Over 300 volunteers—from senior citizen groups to high school ensembles to hula troupes—are part of its "strolling musicians program." Between 10:00 A.M. and 2:00 P.M., these folks are likely to perform at gates where passengers arrive.

The nonprofit council has teamed up with Kapi'olani Community College's Hospitality Department to give customer service training to thousands of airport employees, from security guards to greeters. In cooperation with the Guitar Institute of Hawai'i, it offers 'ukulele and hula lessons to airport employees and their families. And with the assistance of the state's Department of Transportation, it has revived the Honolulu International Airport's newslet-

Ho'okipa Aloha Council volunteers share their aloha with visitors.

ter, called the *Ho'okipa Express,* to keep the airport community updated on news and events.

But the Aloha Council is known most for its public appearances. In September, you are likely to see the Aloha Festivals' Royal Court, dressed in traditional garb, roaming the airport. In December, the Honolulu Boy Choir could make a special appearance. Arriving in Hawai'i should be a memorable experience, and the Aloha Council definitely helps make it so.

**Address: 400 Rodgers Boulevard, Suite 700 Honolulu, Hawai'i 96819
Phone: 838-8040**

▍ THE MUSIC OF HAWAI'I

From 1935 to 1975, the "Hawai'i Calls" program linked the listeners of more than 600 radio stations (at its peak) around the world to Hawai'i and lured many of them here for vacations as well. The "Hawai'i Calls" name lives on as part of Hula Records, the oldest and largest distributor of Hawaiian music in the world. Original recordings by music legends such as Pua Almeida, Alfred Apaka, Charles K.L. Davis, Haunani Kahalewai and Nina Kealiiwahamana are still available via email at hularec@lava.net.

Keith and Carmen Haugen bring Hawaiian music to live radio and Internet audiences.

Worldwide radio networks are gone, but the World Wide Web is taking their place. From 1:00 to 4:00 P.M. every Sunday, Keith and Carmen Haugen host "The Music of Hawai'i" on the Hawai'i public radio stations KIPO 89.3 FM and KIFO 1380 AM. It's also possible for you to hear KIPO at www.hawaiipublicradio.org.

"The Music of Hawai'i" is not quite "Hawai'i Calls" reborn. Gone are the live audiences and the lovely beachside locations. Gone are the live performances. Keith and Carmen record the show in a small studio using both old recordings and many that have been re-released on CD.

The Haugens have one of the world's greatest Hawaiian music collections, and between them boast a near encyclopedic knowledge of Hawaiian music and entertainers. This forms the basis for a show that unveils the heart and soul of Island music.

Carmen comes to Hawaiian music and hula by birth. She was born on Maui into a Hawaiian-Chinese-Filipino-Spanish family. Keith is a Mainlander of Norwegian stock who has become a Hawaiian language teacher and a composer.

They have been a duo, on stage and off, for nearly thirty years, performing at some of the premier venues in Waikīkī and around the world. Their "home" since 1986 has been The Royal Hawaiian hotel, where they perform two nights a week.

Address: The Royal Hawaiian
2259 Kalākaua Avenue
Honolulu, Hawai'i 96815
Phone: 923-7311
Hours: 5:30 to 8:30 P.M. Tuesday and
Wednesday
Web site: www.hawaiiansong.com

▌ THE QUEEN'S SONGBOOK

The term "long awaited" takes on new meaning when applied to *The Queen's Songbook*. In 1897, Lili'uokalani, Hawai'i's last queen, prepared for publication a manuscript she called "He Buke Mele Hawai'i," containing 110 of her songs, melodies and English translations of her work (she was an accomplished composer and songwriter). The monarchy had only recently been overthrown, and the queen deposed. The book was never published, and the queen died in 1917.

Hui Hānai, an auxiliary of the Queen Lili'uokalani Children's Center, set out in 1973 to publish a book that would perpetuate the queen's memory and musical legacy. Twenty-six years later, on Lili'uokalani's birthday, September 2, *The Queen's Songbook* was finally released. It contains fifty-five songs by the queen, including forty-two never before published and five closely associated with her. In addition to songs, the book includes an essay on

Portrait of Lili'uokalani, Hawai'i's last queen.

Lili'uokalani; photographs of her; and music, historical commentary and chronologies.

The Queen's Songbook is unique in many ways. For one, dozens of Hawaiian music luminaries, composers and historians contributed to the book. Many have since passed away, and with them a body of knowledge about Hawai'i and its musical history also has quietly slipped away.

For another, the songbook contains the mo'olelo or "stories behind the songs." "The queen's music is filled with kaona, or hidden meanings, known to those who speak Hawaiian and those who have lived through the experiences her music captures," says Maile Meyer, president of Native Books, which helps distribute the volume. "The research that went into understanding the queen's music provides all of us as readers with an opportunity to share her sources of comfort, pride and intimacy."

Phone: Hui Hānai, 955-5256

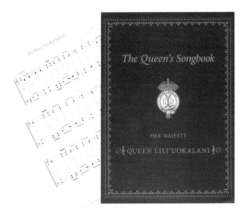

WAIKĪKĪ, IN THE WAKE OF DREAMS

Millions of visitors come each year to Waikīkī—the world's most famous resort—to enjoy its wonderful contradictions. It's a combination of grace and gaudiness, calm and cacophony, beauty and beastly traffic.

Hawai'i-born filmmaker Edgy Lee captures it all in a wonderful documentary entitled *Waikīkī, In the Wake of Dreams*, released in 2001. One of the film's first showings was an open-air screening on Kūhiō Beach, under a full moon in Waikīkī.

In the film, Waikīkī's most famous entertainer, Don Ho, tells how he sometimes walks the beach at night. He pretends that all the hotels are gone and the mile-long crescent of sand and surf is as pristine as the image that has drawn visitors here for over a century.

Take off your shoes and take the same walk yourself. Imagine Waikīkī before Westerners arrived on O'ahu; back then, it was a quiet beachside community with taro and rice farms.

Hawaiian royalty loved to vacation there, as do nearly five million visitors today.

Lee's interviews range from academicians to beachboys. She tells the story of Waikīkī through the musicians who entertained there, the Hollywood stars who escaped there and the movies that were made there. You learn how the advent of air travel in the 1960s spawned the boom in hotel development, reintroducing Waikīkī as a world-class resort.

You also can read *Waikīkī, In the Wake of Dreams*, an attractive 125-page coffee table book written by Lee and Paul Berry. A Warner Reprise CD soundtrack features some of the music from the film.

Address: FilmWorks, P.O. Box 61281
Honolulu, Hawai'i 96839
Phone: 585-9005
Web site: www.filmworkspacific.com

The Hawai'i Visitors & Convention Bureau's Web site contains
detailed information and beautiful images of all the islands.

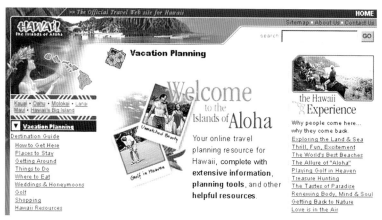

An attractive page from gohawaii.com's site.

The Internet has revolutionized the travel industry. Today, most hotels, retail outlets, activity outfitters and attractions have Web sites, and while you may not yet be booking a flight or hotel or rental car on-line, chances are you will do research on the World Wide Web before going on a trip.

For Hawai'i, the most remote group of islands on Earth, the World Wide Web is a special blessing, connecting it to the world and vice versa. With people of Hawaiian ancestry and people who love Hawai'i dispersed to the four corners of the globe, the Internet is a great connector.

As more and more Island radio stations broadcast their programs and even live concerts on the Internet, there soon will be no place on Earth that you can't find live Hawaiian music. Those working to preserve the Hawaiian culture and language took to the Internet quickly, establishing bulletin boards, all-Hawaiian Web sites, even dictionaries. If you want to translate a word from Hawaiian to English or vice versa, go to www.olelo.hawaii.edu/OP/dictionary/mamaka.html.

The Hawai'i Visitors & Convention Bureau (HVCB) was among the first to see the value of a presence on the World Wide Web. Although their impressive site has not technically been entered in Keep It Hawai'i (it'd be a bit awkward for the HVCB to seek recognition in a program it's sponsoring, after all), we'll take a look at it in this chapter, along with those of a few companies that are unique in that they exist only on the Web. Although these businesses don't have an actual office, you can visit them on-line any time of the day or night.

▥ WWW.GOHAWAII.COM

While the Hawai'i Visitors & Convention Bureau has seen changes and evolved since its inception in 1892, it has remained steadfast in its commitment to be at the forefront of global destination marketing.

The Internet is playing an increasingly significant role in travel marketing and sales. HVCB's gohawaii.com Web site is at the vanguard of destination sites, and is an essential part of Hawai'i's integrated marketing strategies.

Gohawaii.com is a sophisticated Web system that serves as *the* portal for access to all Hawai'i destination information, products and services. It is a fully integrated platform that serves the global needs of HVCB, its Island Chapters and members.

In addition, gohawaii.com is a communications channel that attracts a broad user group with diverse demographics and interests. And it is a fun and easy on-line experience that exceeds expectations and motivates travel to the world's most desired destination—Hawai'i, The Islands of Aloha.

■ WWW.CHINATOWNHI.COM

Honolulu's Chinatown may not be as large as San Francisco's or New York's, but it is every bit as exotic. Intriguing shops, open-air markets, ornate temples, hole-in-the-wall restaurants and mysterious alleyways are all to be found there.

Before you go, check out chinatownhi.com to make your visit much more meaningful. Learn about Chinatown's 200-year history and its cultural traditions. Download a map and

take a virtual tour. Click on the cookie for your fortune. You can even link to Chinatowns around the world.

The site intensifies your Chinatown experience with the writings of those who know it well, including a poem by local bard Wing Tek Lum and fascinating Chinatown tales by travel writer Rick Carroll. Run by the Pacific Information Exchange, chinatownhi.com also fills other needs. Via e-mail, people can ask about tour guides, jade jewelry repairs, nearby hotels, specific dates for celebrations and parades, and how to have a wedding in Chinatown and arrange a traditional lion dance for a function.

The most hits come during Chinese holidays. Many site visitors are homesick Islanders. When you have finished your visit to Chinatown, you can add your own observations at chinatownhi.com. Most poignant are pleas from people in China who are desperate to get out of the country.

■ WWW.E808.COM

Several tech-savvy young Hawai'i residents who were homesick college kids on the Mainland created e808.com, "Hawai'i's first pure Internet start-up dedicated to its unique lifestyle," in July 1999.

The site is an on-line catalog filled with 2,000-plus locally-made wares from over fifty well-respected vendors, including apparel, books, music, food, jewelry, arts and crafts, surfing gear and more that would usually only be found within the state. For the visitor who missed the chance to buy some desired Island product, for the former resident who longs for local merchandise, for college students yearning for a taste of home, e808.com offers a place to get a quick Hawaiian fix.

Log into e808.com and enjoy the breezy, happy-go-lucky attitude that you expect from Hawai'i college kids. Its listing of top sellers is a great guide to what's hot and what's not in the Islands, from board shorts to bumper stickers—"Got poi?", "Got aloha?", "Got surf?" Get it?

The site also offers displaced Islanders a newsletter and links to sites like hawaiiclubs.org, a listing of Hawai'i clubs at colleges across the nation. The founders of e808.com have carved out a niche as a premier on-line site for Island lifestyle products, and shared a lot of fun, too.

▌▌ WWW.HAWAII.COM

Reaching out to residents, visitors, anyone moving to Hawai'i and everyone dreaming about Hawai'i, Hawaii.com is an Internet portal that aspires to be the Hawai'i "everything" site.

Hawaii.com has one of the easiest Web addresses to remember, and it offers quick access to the sites of its community partners: the state of Hawai'i; Hawai'i Visitors & Convention Bureau; University of Hawai'i; Office of Hawaiian Affairs; City and County of Honolulu; County of Maui; County of Kaua'i; KHNL News 8, the local NBC affiliate; KFVE, which televises University of Hawai'i sports; Hawai'i Public Radio; the Pacific Basin Economic Council; Hawai'i Museums Association; and Aloha United Way, a nonprofit organization that supports over sixty-five local charities.

Hawaii.com's Lū'au! Section was inspired by questions from visitors to the site. It is a reference spot where you can learn about the

Ha'ena Beach, Kaua'i
Peter French ©HVCB

cultural significance and customs of the lū'au before attending a commercial or private one in the Islands. You'll find out how to prepare lū'au dishes, how to dig an imu or underground oven, and where you can buy lū'au supplies on-line. The site even describes games that were played in ancient times that you can re-create at your own Hawaiian feast.

◼ WWW.RODEOHAWAII.COM

You may not realize that Hawai'i's paniolo (cowboy) lifestyle preceded the American West's cowboy culture by almost forty years. In 1793, British Captain George Vancouver presented King Kamehameha with five longhorn cows that he had obtained at the Spanish mission of Monterey in California. A decade later, the king received two horses as gifts from Richard J. Cleveland, the American captain of the brig *Lelia Byrd*.

Allowed to roam freely in the wilderness region above Waimea on the Big Island, the royal herd of cattle multiplied beyond control. In 1832, recognizing he needed to resolve the situation, King Kamehameha III brought vaqueros from California to teach the Hawaiians how to ride horses and round up cattle. The word "paniolo" is a derivative of *espanola,* meaning Spanish.

In 1908, Parker Ranch paniolo Ikua Purdy won the World Rodeo Steer Roping Championship at Frontier Days in Cheyenne, Wyoming— and a coveted place in Island history. At that prestigious event, the Hawaiians proved they not only could ride the waves, they could ride horses!

The Hawai'i Island Economic Development Board created the Paniolo Hawaiian Cowboy Project in response to a "stampeding" interest in Hawai'i's cowboy heritage. Its Web site, rodeohawaii.com, tells the story of the paniolo, from olden times to modern days. It describes the attire, language and music of the Hawaiian cowboy, who, with his 'ukulele and lei-bedecked Stetson, cuts a distinctive figure on the range, indeed.

Rodeohawaii.com also lists the ranches, outfitters, retail outlets and organizations that help perpetuate the Islands' unique paniolo heritage. A calendar of events, including rodeos held statewide, is regularly updated on the Web site.

Two other excellent sources of information are Edgy Lee's Kahili Award-winning video, "Na Paniolo o Hawai'i," and the accompanying CD, "Songs of the Hawaiian Cowboy, Na Mele o Paniolo."

Embraced by lush gardens and cool trade winds, Hawai'i Calls
Restaurant at the Big Island's Outrigger Waikoloa Beach Resort
sets the mood for a memorable evening.

FACING   FUTURE

IZ
ISRAEL
KAMAKAWIWOʻOLE

Eye-catching cover of one of the Mountain Apple Company's most popular releases.

In 1999, the Hawaiʻi Visitors & Convention Bureau added a new Keep It Hawaiʻi award to honor companies that have gone "above and beyond the call" of doing business in the Islands. These are businesses, large and small, that have in some way made a special commitment and contribution to Hawaiʻi and its all-important visitor industry.

The honor is called the Pōmaikaʻi Award, and it pays tribute to O Ka ʻOihana I Hana Pōmaikaʻi, which is Hawaiian for "The Business That Creates Good Fortune." These are firms whose investment and commitment to Hawaiʻi's future help to create jobs and promote the travel industry.

These companies are usually familiar by name to Island residents, but often the complete story of their contributions may not be as well-known. Visitors probably aren't aware at all about the behind-the-scenes efforts of these businesses (and others that will receive the award in years to come).

These Pōmaikaʻi winners are a vital part of the experience that makes Hawaiʻi one of the most popular travel destinations in the world.

CONTINENTAL AIRLINES

Continental Airlines has a long history in the Pacific. Its first service between Hawai'i and the Mainland began in September 1969. Even before that, Air Micronesia, Continental's subsidiary, connected the Islands to their neighbors in the Western Pacific.

Continental's commitment and confidence in Hawai'i has been demonstrated again and again. Recently, it built a major aircraft maintenance facility in Hawai'i, employing hundreds of people in construction and long-term high-tech work—a welcome boost to the local economy.

As a firmly grounded part of the local community, Continental became a sponsor of aviation and aerospace education at the University of Hawai'i and regularly contributes to good causes, like community theater, in the

Continental Airlines wins kudos for its contributions to Hawai'i.

Islands. It regularly ranks among the nation's top airlines in customer satisfaction, and is listed in the top twenty-five of *Fortune* magazine's "100 Best Companies to Work for in America."

Continental sponsors a Congress of Chefs, composed of celebrity chefs from around the country who serve as consultants to the airline in the area of food preparation. The Congress includes Hawai'i-based Roy Yamaguchi, whose Roy's restaurants have been at the forefront in promoting Hawai'i Regional Cuisine around the world. Continental also has a global partner relationship with Hawaiian Airlines, Hawai'i's oldest airline, which launched interisland flights in 1929.

Most important, Continental Airlines has assumed a leadership role in inaugurating new flights to the Islands, boosting capacity on existing routes and incorporating Hawaiian culture on its flights.

A Continental Airlines customer service representative assists visitors.

**Address: 735 Bishop Street, Suite 235
Honolulu, Hawai'i 96813
Phone: 532-5005
Web site: www.continental.com**

OUTRIGGER HOTELS & RESORTS

Outrigger Hotels & Resorts is Hawai'i's largest hotel group and the most prominent group that is owned and headquartered here. Its history is an amazing story of hard work and dedication to values like family and community service.

When Roy and Estelle Kelley arrived in the Islands in 1929, hotels in Waikīkī catered to the well-heeled set. Kelley, an architect, began his career developing small apartment buildings in Waikīkī. In 1947, the Kelleys opened their first hotel, the fifty-room Islander, offering lodging at moderate prices (and the first self-operating elevator) in Waikīkī.

After jet travel began in 1959, their business boomed. Kelley built the seventeen-story Reef, the first high-rise on Waikīkī Beach, in 1955. In those days, he was the designer, engineer, contractor, administrator and often financier for the company. He and Estelle worked long hours, seven days a week, sometimes doing menial jobs—whatever it took to get things done.

In 1963, lease talks with another company for the original Outrigger Canoe Club property on Waikīkī Beach stalemated, and Kelley swiftly put his own offer on the table. The property became the site of the flagship Outrigger Waikīkī, and the rest of Kelley's hotel chain was reborn with the Outrigger name.

Roy and Estelle Kelley (who both passed away in the late 1990s) gradually turned over the reins of the company to their son Richard, who left his medical practice to take charge. Richard is now Outrigger's very active chair-

Roy and Estelle Kelley founded Outrigger Hotels & Resorts, Hawai'i's largest hotel group. This photo of the couple was taken around 1950.

man of the board. His son-in-law, David Carey, runs the company as president and chief executive officer, and many other family members work at various levels of the enterprise.

Today, the company's over three dozen properties are divided in two divisions—deluxe full-service Outrigger resorts and OHANA hotels for the budget conscious. There currently are Outrigger hotels in Guam, Fiji, the Marshall Islands and Australia, and the company plans to introduce the Outrigger name in other regions of the Pacific as well.

As a homegrown, family-run concern, the "Kelleys of the Outrigger" have helped shape tourism in the Islands, bringing "The Outrigger Way" of hospitality to millions of visitors and helping to keep the aloha spirit and Hawaiian traditions alive.

Address: 2375 Kūhiō Avenue
Honolulu, Hawai'i 96815
Phone: 921-6600
Web site: www.outrigger.com

■ MOUNTAIN APPLE COMPANY

No music has traveled farther or brought more travelers to its source than Hawaiian music.

Directed by Chief Executive Officer Jon de Mello, the Mountain Apple Company has been a giant in the Hawaiian music industry. Since it was founded in 1947, it has published, produced, recorded, distributed and staged performances of Hawaiian music by over 400 top local performers.

Mountain Apple's artists and their music touch the lives of Hawai'i residents and visitors every day, from the recorded music that fills our airwaves to live shows like the Brothers Cazimero's annual Lei Day concert on May 1, which has been going strong for over twenty years. Mountain Apple also broadens the reach of Hawaiian music "beyond the reef," as de Mello says, licensing music worldwide for television, films, music videos and broadcast advertising.

Take the incredible story of Israel Kamakawiwo'ole, known to much of the world simply as "IZ." The 800-pound 'ukulele-playing legend passed away at age thirty-eight in 1997, the year his music spent a record thirty-nine weeks on *Billboard* magazine's Top World Music Chart.

IZ's sweet, simple rendition of "Over The Rainbow/What A Wonderful World" brought a huge following to Hawaiian music. It was featured in the film *Meet Joe Black* with Brad Pitt and *Finding Forrester* with Sean Connery, and was the theme music for the eToys.com on-line toy company.

In collaboration with the Bishop Museum, Mountain Apple released a CD of chants and songs from the turn of the century that were originally recorded on wax cylinders. Another CD, *Kekuhi,* by the Big Island's Kekuhi Kanahele, was released in an all-Hawaiian text edition with liner notes, song notes and even credits in the Hawaiian language.

Mountain Apple has combined devotion to cultural preservation and enhancement with commercial success. Its recordings are available wherever Hawaiian music is sold, including the World Wide Web.

Address: P.O. Box 22373
Honolulu, Hawai'i 96823
Phone: 597-1888
Web site: www.mountainapplecompany.com

The Mountain Apple Company's offerings include both traditional and contemporary Hawaiian music.

PLEASANT HAWAIIAN HOLIDAYS
ED AND LYNN HOGAN

Ed and Lynn Hogan began Pleasant Travel Service, a small travel agency in New Jersey, in 1959, the year Hawai'i became a state. Ed Hogan first came to the Islands in 1954 as a pilot with Trans Ocean Air Lines, which offered the first group tours to Hawai'i.

Ed and Lynn Hogan are leaders in the Hawaiian–and global–travel industry.

In 1962, the Hogans launched Pleasant Hawaiian Holidays in California, specializing in attractively priced package tours to Hawai'i. The tours were a huge success, and today, Pleasant Hawaiian is a $400-million company that employs more than 1,700 people. The firm owns four hotels, and operates its own scheduled airline charter service. It spends as much as $12 million a year on Hawai'i promotions, and at last count had brought more than five million visitors to the Islands, with the number growing by 500,000 a year.

For his contributions to tourism, Ed has received many honors, including earning a coveted spot in the Travel Industry Association's Hall of Leaders and being ranked among *Tour & Travel News'* Most Influential Executives in the Tour and Travel Industry. The Hogans have been inducted into the American Society of Travel Agents' World Travel Hall of Fame.

In 1987, Hawai'i's State Senate proclaimed Ed Hogan "Mr. Tourism." The next year, Ed, Lynn and their children set up the Hogan Family Foundation, a nonprofit organization "dedicated to promoting a greater understanding of the importance of travel and tourism within our society."

The Hogan family's philanthropy has focused primarily on education, including providing scholarships to many Hawai'i students of travel and tourism. They recently funded the Ed and Lynn Hogan Program in Travel and Tourism at Loyola Marymount University in Los Angeles, California to prepare students for future careers in the industry.

In 1999, when Kodak pulled out as a sponsor, the Hogan Family Foundation stepped forward to save the popular free Kodak Hula Show, which had been a well-loved institution in Waikīkī since 1937. Now called the Pleasant Hawaiian Hula Show, it continues to delight audiences three times a week at the Waikīkī Shell.

**Address: 1601 Kapi'olani Boulevard, Suite 960
Honolulu, Hawai'i 96814
Phone: 945-1800
Web site: www.pleasantholidays.com**

With the help of Chevron Hawaiʻi, the endangered aeʻo,
or Hawaiian stilt, has found a safe haven.

**Detail of a fifty-foot Hawaiian-themed mural at the
JW Marriott 'Ihilani Resort & Spa.**

The first thing most people fall in love with in Hawai'i is its incredible beauty. The towering green mountains, silvery waterfalls, crescents of white sand, gorgeous blue-green ocean and thick groves of nodding palms are the dreams of Island travelers come true.

Everyone knows that Hawai'i's allure and its economic well-being depend on the health of its environment. And like anywhere else on Earth where humans reside, Hawai'i faces its challenges in this regard.

It is already the endangered species center of the world, and alien species, whether introduced on purpose or by accident, are a continuing danger. Environmentalists in the Islands are concerned about everything from the availability of water to the disposal of rubbish.

The Environmental Preservation category of Keep It Hawai'i recognizes efforts—both large and small—by companies to protect and improve the Islands' fragile environment. Here are some champions of the cause.

CHEVRON HAWAIʻI

In a chapter about environmental preservation, it might seem strange to highlight an oil company. But Chevron's story is worth telling because preserving Hawaiʻi's delicate ecosystem is everyone's business.

In 1992, Chevron Hawaiʻi Refinery employees noticed many black-necked birds with long, slender legs nesting at a six-acre catchment pond among the oil tanks of its Kapolei Refinery in west Oʻahu. The uninvited birds were identified as the aeʻo or endangered Hawaiian stilt. One option was to drain the pond and cover the area with nets, driving the aeʻo away.

Instead, the company teamed with the U.S. Fish and Wildlife Service to transform the pond into an endangered species reserve. To make the pond similar to the birds' natural wetlands habitat, water is maintained at the optimum level and quality.

Chevron managers and employees have adopted the aeʻo as their unofficial mascot and protect the eggs and hatchlings in many ways,

Ten percent of the surviving aeʻo in Hawaiʻi make their home at Rowland's Pond.

including trapping and removing cats and mongooses—the birds' primary predators. Thanks to Chevron's education program about the aeʻo, all employees ensure the birds are not distressed in any way.

Through the efforts of Chevron and its people, more than 300 aeʻo hatchlings have reached maturity in nine years. Now, nearly ten percent of the surviving aeʻo in Hawaiʻi call Rowland's Pond at the Chevron Hawaiʻi Refinery home.

Tours are arranged for school and community groups and environmental organizations to see the aeʻo and the endangered Hawaiian coots that also live at the refinery. During nesting season, the tour schedule is adjusted so as not to disturb the birds. You can arrange a tour by calling Chevron's Hawaiʻi corporate office, or pay a virtual visit to the pond via the company's Web site.

Address: 91-480 Malakole Street
Kapolei, Hawaiʻi 96707
Phone: 682-2216
Web site: www.chevron.com/environment/
peopledo/CPDHawaii.html

An aeʻo chick born at Rowland's Pond.

■ FAIR WIND CRUISES

Since 1971, the Dant family has owned and operated Fair Wind, an ocean adventures business that has brought thousands of visitors to pristine Kealakekua Bay on the Big Island's South Kona Coast.

The bay is a marine sanctuary with abundant tropical fish and a variety of coral reefs that are usually visible to 100 feet in depth. At one end of the bay, a simple white monument marks the spot where Captain James Cook met his demise in 1779. For its historical significance and snorkeling and scuba opportunities, Kealakekua Bay is a fabulous place to visit.

What sets Fair Wind Cruises apart is a fierce commitment to environmental preservation. Its owners and crew are always on the

The *Fair Wind* approaches the Captain Cook Memorial in Kealakekua Bay.

watch for debris in the bay. Fair Wind educates its customers about Kealakekua Bay's precious coral reef and marine life, and stresses careful, low-impact use of the bay.

The sixty-foot customized catamaran, *Fair Wind,* is equipped with a special oil filter to prevent discharges into the bay and a "manta mooring system" that minimizes damage to the coral reef.

The Dants also have financially supported a joint project with the Waikīkī Aquarium and the state's Division of Aquatic Resources to replant coral from abundant sites in damaged areas of the bay. Their efforts have been worthwhile; new coral growth continues to be detected.

Fair Wind Cruises' primary goals are to protect the environment and provide a quality recreational experience for its guests. Photo by Michael Darden.

**Address: 78-7130 Kaleiopapa Street
Kailua-Kona, Hawai'i 96740
Phone: 322-2788
Web site: www.fair-wind.com**

■ HILTON WAIKOLOA VILLAGE

On the barren Kohala Coast of the Big Island, the 1,240-room Hilton Waikoloa Village is an expansive oasis. Canal boats and monorails carry visitors from the lobby to their hotel towers, passing man-made waterfalls and pools, a multimillion-dollar collection of Asian and Pacific art, and lush landscaping. In a word, the resort is spectacular.

It is amazing, then, to learn that without much fanfare, Waikoloa Village has garnered awards for environmental preservation. When the resort added an eighteen-hole putting course, it became an educational opportunity for guests to see, touch and smell plants native to Hawai'i. Among the Seaside Putting Course's collection of carefully maintained and marked plants are the ma'o, the relatively rare indigenous Hawaiian cotton plant with a beautiful yellow blossom, and 'ūlei, a spreading shrub that's strong and flexible enough to be used for fishnets.

As you ride the canal boats, be sure to look in the water around you. In 1999, Waikoloa Village started to create a reef habitat, complete with tropical fish and invertebrates, in the mile-long waterway stretching across the sixty-two-acre resort. To make this educational project work, it created an on-site marine life quaran-

Excited youngsters meet one of the Hilton Waikoloa Village's friendly dolphins.

tine facility. It voluntarily collected its stock at remote, unpopular diving areas and took great care so that not a single specimen was lost due to stress going through the quarantine facility.

As a result, the Hilton Waikoloa Village Waterway Project has set the industry standard by which all similar projects will be measured in the future, according to the state's Division of Aquatic Resources. "Its positive impact on environmental conservation through education will have a lasting value for the promotion of Hawai'i's tourism industry for years to come."

Address: 425 Waikoloa Beach Drive
Waikoloa, Hawai'i 96738
Phone: 886-1234
Web site: www.hiltonwaikoloavillage.com

■ 'IHILANI RESORT AND SPA

Many companies paper their walls with mottoes and mission statements. 'Ihilani Resort and Spa (now the JW Marriott 'Ihilani Resort and Spa) took signage to a higher level and turned its commitment to environmental preservation into an inspirational fifty-foot mural that adorns the employee entrance to the award-winning resort.

To paint the mural, art students from nearby Nānākuli High School were enlisted to help. The resort has a "School to Work" partnership with Nānākuli High, and donates all its recycled aluminum—500 pounds a year—to the school to raise funds to buy computers.

"Our tourism industry relies on Hawai'i's natural beauty to attract visitors," says the JW Marriott 'Ihilani's General Manager John Homer. "We believe it is our responsibility to preserve and protect Hawai'i's beauty by reducing the environmental impact of our operations."

That means recycling all glass, aluminum and food waste; recycling energy between air-cooling and hot-water systems; and saving water with ultra-low flow toilets and shower

The ancient Hawaiians had a special relationship with the land, ocean, flora and fauna that sustained them.

heads. The resort even uses a conservation-conscious method to create chlorine for its two swimming pools. Machines called electonators convert salt to chlorine gas, eliminating the need to buy or store toxic chemicals.

The hotel's employees continue to find creative ways to meet the resort's environmental mission. The grass for a new nine-hole putting green was generated from cuttings using techniques that required less water and enabled the grass to sprout more quickly than if it had been planted from seeds. Sand, compost and crumbled auto tire rubber were mixed and laid over the ground to prevent soil compaction. Unwanted grass and shrubs were saved and replanted in another location on the resort grounds. Even the park benches are made from recycled plastics.

**Address: 92-1001 'Ōlani Street
Kapolei, Hawai'i 96707
Phone: 679-0079
Web site: marriott.com**

Neighborhood high school students donated their talents to the mural project.

■ MOLOKA'I RANCH

Moloka'i Ranch, Hawai'i's second-largest ranch, has a royal heritage; it once belonged to King Kamehameha V. During the last century, it has been a cattle ranch and pineapple plantation, but starting in 1986, when the last pineapple-growing operation left Moloka'i, its focus began to change.

On its 54,000 acres (more than a third of the island), Moloka'i Ranch has created an "adventure" destination that allows visitors to enjoy nature and an uncommon Hawaiian experience with only modest impact on the environment, culture and society of this special place.

The ranch's seaside accommodations are low-impact, simple and environmentally sensitive. Each tentalow (tent on a bungalow frame) has solar-powered electricity and water heaters, self-composting toilets and waste recycling to promote environmental sensitivity and protect the countryside.

One of Moloka'i Ranch's most popular cultural activities is a hike led by a knowledgeable Islander who interprets ancient sites and petroglyphs on ranch land and explains how the people of old lived and worked on the island. Similarly, other activities complement Moloka'i's rich culture and history. For example, you can kayak to ancient fishponds, mount a horse and ride on cattle trails with real cowboys, cycle to tidal pools and scenic overlooks, and paddle an outrigger canoe just like the Hawaiians of old did.

At Moloka'i Ranch, your pace and pulse will slow. Put away your watch. You won't need it. When you stay here, you'll learn to live life according to the rhythms of nature.

Hawaiian history and important archaeological sites are unveiled during hikes at Moloka'i Ranch.

Address: 100 Maunaloa Highway
Maunaloa, Hawai'i 96770
Phone: 534-9579
Web site: www.molokairanch.com

■ SHERATON HOTELS HAWAI'I

For a decade, Sheraton Hotels in Hawai'i have found that it is good business being green—in the best environmental sense. Its four O'ahu hotels—Sheraton Waikīkī, Sheraton Moana Surfrider, Sheraton Princess Ka'iulani and The Royal Hawaiian—comprise 4,200 guest rooms or thirteen percent of the rooms in Waikīkī. Thus, the company has had a major impact on the environment of Hawai'i's premier visitor destination and all of O'ahu.

Sheraton has been a leader in caring for Hawai'i's environment, and its Resource Management Program has been recognized with over a dozen awards, including the Partnership for the Environment's Outstanding Service Award in New Recycling Systems and Technology.

Sheraton has found that more than half of guest-room waste is recyclable. Each month, it recycles more than fifty tons of waste; glass, cardboard, paper, aluminum, newsprint, wooden pallets, printer cartridges, used cooking oil and food scraps are sorted at the central loading dock and sent on to a second life.

The other half of environmental awareness is using materials after recycling. Sheraton prints most of its materials on recycled paper, and its laundry and utility bags are made from recycled plastic. Toiletries are packed in recycled paperboard. Most likely your pillowcase was a sheet in its previous life, before it got ripped but not ruined. And on it goes.

Sheraton's environmental program has resulted in savings of $100,000 a year and has ac-

The Sheraton Waikīkī has been a leader in employing sound environmental practices.

tually created jobs. Along with ever-important water conservation, the program has meant a Hawai'i that is a better place to live—and to visit.

Sheraton Moana Surfrider (922-3111)
Address: 2365 Kalākaua Avenue
Honolulu, Hawai'i 96815

Sheraton Princess Ka'iulani (922-5811)
Address: 120 Ka'iulani Avenue
Honolulu, Hawai'i 96815

Sheraton Waikīkī (922-4422)
Address: 2255 Kalākaua Avenue
Honolulu, Hawai'i 96815

The Royal Hawaiian (923-7311)
Address: 2259 Kalākaua Avenue
Honolulu, Hawai'i 96815

Web site: www.sheraton-hawaii.com

■ VOLCANO ART CENTER

At the 3,800-foot elevation in Volcano on the Big Island, there's a native rain forest that a dedicated group is determined to save. In 1997, the Volcano Art Center leased 7.4 acres from the state of Hawai'i to build classrooms, offices and studio space, and to restore the native forest at Niaulani in Volcano Village.

Niaulani means "brushed by the heavens," after the mist and billowing clouds that blow across the treetops in the rain forest. "For years I watched in dismay as this remnant native rain forest was invaded by alien plants, threatening the survival of old-growth trees and destroying the rich understory," said Jon Giffin, the state's forestry manager for the area.

One of the first things the Volcano Art Center did was conduct an extensive survey of the site followed by a model forest management plan to enhance and preserve the native forest vegetation. Pretty but threatening Asian flowering plants like tibouchina and Himalayan raspberry were choking the native forest. Now, tall koa and 'ōhi'a trees preside over the forest, while beneath them restored and revived native plants flourish, from the rare meu fern to the mountain naupaka to the ginseng-like 'ōlapa, whose fluttering leaves emulate the graceful gestures of a hula dancer.

With help from the Keākealani Outdoor Education Center, thousands of schoolchildren have visited Niaulani. Adults come, too, and are assisted on their tours through the forest by an illustrated plant guide that can be downloaded in advance from the Volcano Art Center's Web site.

Shunning artificial herbicides and using only organic fertilizers, volunteers do most of the work at Niaulani. Invasive plants are removed by hand and composted. Native plants are propagated on the site, and six times a year propagation workshops are offered.

Today, as you walk through the rain forest, you will be amazed not only by its majestic trees and native shrubs, but by the songs of native birds like the 'apapane, 'elepaio, 'amakihi and ōma'o. Niaulani is alive once again.

Address: P.O. Box 104
Hawai'i Volcanoes National Park, Hawai'i 96718
Phone: 967-8222
Web site: www.volcanoartcenter.org

Children who visit Niaulani are encouraged to plant native flora in the forest and leave a wooden plaque to mark their gift.

A beautiful "bouquet" of coral at the Maui Ocean Center.
Photo by Stratus.

It's snack time for a sea lion at the Waikīkī Aquarium.

For years, Hawai'i's television stations had no weatherpersons. Except for occasional storms and very rare hurricanes, local weather reports sound remarkably the same. In fact, Island residents recognize only two seasons. Winter, from about mid-October through April, is cool and wet, with less dependable trade winds. Summer, May through mid-October, is warm and dry with steadier trades and, of course, longer days.

When it comes to weather in the Aloha State, geography is a more important factor than time of year. Hawai'i has microclimates, with clear differences evident between the shores and plains at sea level and the mountains and valleys that rise steeply above them. The windward sides of the Islands are wetter and windier than the leeward sides.

Rarely is semitropical Hawai'i not immersed in sunshine, meaning you can wear shorts and sleeveless shirts pretty much all year round. The Islands' balmy weather enables you to indulge in a host of pleasurable activities, including ocean sports, golf, tennis, jogging, biking and horseback riding.

Most of Hawai'i's attractions also lure you outdoors. This chapter spotlights options that go out of their way to offer unique cultural, historical and ecological experiences.

◼ ALEXANDER & BALDWIN SUGAR MUSEUM

Today, tourism is king, but once upon a time King Sugar ruled the Hawaiian economy.

The possibility of growing sugarcane for profit gave the land that once ultimately all belonged to the king great value to outsiders. The water needed to grow the cane made water rights an extremely valuable commodity as well. And the need for people to work the cane fields led sugar growers to import a succession of Asian and European laborers. These immigrants intermingled and intermarried, so that Hawai'i's population today is a wonderful cosmopolitan mix that James Michener called "the golden people" in his epic novel, *Hawai'i.*

Sugar has played a key role in Hawai'i's economy. In 1869, Samuel Alexander and Henry Baldwin, sons of Lahaina missionaries, purchased twelve acres of cane land below Makawao. This was the beginning of what today is Alexander & Baldwin, Inc., one of Hawai'i's leading diversified corporations.

The nonprofit Alexander & Baldwin Sugar Museum on Maui is housed in the former residence of the superintendent of Pu'unēnē Mill, which has been in operation across the street since 1902. The museum has won local, state and national awards for preserving the history and heritage of the sugar industry and the multiethnic plantation life that it engendered.

A 1930 Caterpillar Sixty tractor and a 1956 Euclid cane hauler are among the retired plan-

The history of sugar in Hawai'i comes to life at the Alexander & Baldwin Sugar Museum.

tation field equipment displayed on the museum grounds. Inside, the museum exhibits huge photo murals, authentic scale models and sugar industry artifacts dating back to 1878. The highlight is a working model of sugar mill machinery, which shows how cane is turned into raw sugar while a computer-controlled narrative with special lighting and sound effects explains what is happening.

It's easy to miss the modest building. Look for the tall sugar mill stacks—the most visible landmark in Central Maui—and you will find the Alexander & Baldwin Sugar Museum close by.

**Address: 3957 Hansen Road
Pu'unēnē, Hawai'i 96784
Phone: 871-8058
Hours: 9:30 A.M. to 4:30 P.M. Monday through Saturday. Also open Sunday during February, March, July and August.
Web site: www.sugarmuseum.com**

■ BISHOP MUSEUM

Bishop Museum, officially designated the "State Museum of Natural and Cultural History," has been the leading repository for Polynesian culture for over 100 years. If you are serious about Hawaiian history—or are a compulsive museum aficionado—this is a must stop on O'ahu.

Charles Reed Bishop, an American businessman, founded the museum in honor of his late wife, Princess Bernice Pauahi Bishop, the last descendant of the royal Kamehameha family. When Pauahi died in 1885 she left her husband all her family possessions. Her cousin, Queen Emma, died soon after and bequeathed her heirlooms to Bishop as well.

Today, Bishop Museum is the premier natural and cultural history institution in the Pacific. In addition to personal belongings and papers of many distinguished individuals, including Hawaiian royalty, the museum safeguards 500,000 plant specimens, six million Hawaiian seashells and over a million photographs dating from the first daguerreotype portrait made in Hawai'i in 1847 to images from the present day. It also is the guardian of priceless articles of clothing, weapons, maps, movies, manuscripts, audio recordings and drawings by artists who sailed on European expeditions in the Pacific during the eighteenth century.

Only a small portion of the museum's vast collection is on view at any one time. Displays that always delight include the magnificent feathered capes and adornments of Hawaiian

A grass hale (hut) and a real skeleton of a sperm whale are among the many treasures that can be seen in the museum's Hawaiian Hall.

royalty, carved wooden images of deities and magnificent examples of nineteenth-century Hawaiian quilts, all painstakenly sewn by hand.

Over the years, new buildings have been added to the twelve-acre campus, including an excellent planetarium; the Castle Building, where traveling exhibits are displayed; and Atherton Hālau, a venue for cultural performances and demonstrations.

A variety of tours and programs are offered, the most intriguing one being the behind-the-scenes look at the museum's workrooms, vaults and treasures that are not normally on public display.

Address: 1525 Bernice Street
Honolulu, Hawai'i 96819
Phone: 847-3511
Hours: 9:00 A.M. to 5:00 P.M. daily
except Christmas Day
Web site: www.bishopmuseum.org

■ HAWAI'I MARITIME CENTER

In an age of jet planes, it is easy to forget the role the sea plays in Hawai'i. From the arrival of the earliest Polynesian voyaging canoes, to the days of the whalers and missionaries, to the time when a ship was the only way to go anywhere, the harbor has been our lifeline.

Today, countless vessels bring most of the freight—from toilet paper to trucks—that we use. In recent years, the return of a growing number of great ocean liners is making O'ahu's Honolulu Harbor a hub of visitor activity again as well.

No place in Hawai'i captures all this better than the Hawai'i Maritime Center. Local architect Philip "Pip" K. White's design was inspired by the Myrtle Boat Club, founded in 1883 on the waterfront near the foot of Punchbowl Street close to where King Kalākaua's original boathouse stood.

Housed in the Hawai'i Maritime Center's two-story, 25,000-square-foot wooden building, called the Kalākaua Boat House, is an extensive collection of marine and maritime exhibits, plus a waterfront restaurant and festival space. Its large central window looks out on two historic vessels—*Hōkūle'a*, the first modern double-hulled canoe built using ancient methods, and *The Falls of Clyde*, the only four-masted square-rigged sailing ship still in existence.

One nostalgic exhibit describes what it was like to travel by sea when the Matson Company's ocean liners were the only modes of transportation between Hawai'i and the continental United States. Times haven't really changed all that much. You can walk to Aloha Tower, across the harbor, and see passengers disembarking from modern-day luxury liners, exuberant at the prospect of vacationing in paradise.

Address: Pier 7, Honolulu Harbor
Honolulu, Hawai'i 96813
Phone: 536-6374
Hours: 8:30 A.M. to 5:00 P.M. daily
Web site: www.holoholo.org/maritime

Surfing is part of Hawai'i's love affair with the sea.

■ HAWAI'I TROPICAL BOTANICAL GARDEN

Abundant rainfall and rich volcanic soil make the Hāmākua Coast of the Big Island one of the lushest regions in the state. Plants that struggle in home gardens reach huge proportions here. Hawai'i Tropical Botanical Garden at Onomea Bay provides a wonderful chance to explore the Hawaiian rain forest. Onomea means "the best place," and you will immediately understand how it got its name when you visit.

When Dan J. Lutkenhouse, the owner of a San Francisco trucking company, first visited Onomea Valley, he bought seventeen jungle-

Visitors enjoy the garden's amazing array of plant life.

like acres, not knowing exactly what to do with it. He soon decided to establish a botanical garden, and eventually created a nonprofit foundation to preserve the valley and its beauty.

For eight years before it opened to the public, Lutkenhouse and volunteers cleared the land with hand tools and wheelbarrows to avoid soil runoff. During that time, he discovered a three-tiered waterfall said to be the most beautiful in the state.

Hawai'i Tropical Botanical Garden is committed to preserving rare and endangered Hawaiian plants, but its collection is truly international. Over 2,000 species are found in the pristine forty-acre valley, including enormous mango and coconut palm trees that are over 100 years old.

From the visitor center, you embark on a self-guided tour that's about a mile long. Allow at least two hours for your visit. From the Lily Lake Vista, Lutkenhouse contends more plant species can be seen in one place than anywhere else on Earth. He's counted over 110. But don't take his word for it—count them yourself!

Address: P.O. Box 80
Pāpaikou, Hawai'i 96781
Phone: 964-5233
Hours: 9:00 A.M. to 4:00 P.M.
Monday through Friday
Web site: www.hawaiigarden.com

HAWAIIAN MUSIC HALL OF FAME

Don't look for the Hawaiian Music Hall of Fame and Museum on any map. For now, its exhibits framed in dark koa move around to sites such as the Hawai'i State Library, Kawaiaha'o Church, schools and hotels. You'll have to check its Web site or contact its organizers to find out where you can see its displays at a particular time. Still, the museum is a real place in the hearts and minds of its supporters.

Since its founding in 1995, the Hall of Fame has annually inducted a distinguished group of Hawaiian musicians, composers and vocalists. It is adding biographies of its honorees to its Web site, starting with Keaulumoku, a legendary chanter and prophet who lived from 1716 to 1784.

On the Internet, you also can learn about Nā Lani 'Eha, "The Royal Four": King Kalākaua, his brother Prince William Leleiohoku, and his sisters Queen Lili'uokalani and Princess Miriam Likelike, the patrons of Hawaiian music. Gradually, links to all those honored will offer a resource for schoolchildren and fans around the world.

The Hall of Fame's goal is to create a permanent gathering place where residents and visitors can learn about Hawai'i's great musical and cultural traditions. The driving force be-

Marjorie Scott (left) greets well-wishers at the 1995 induction ceremony, including Michael Chun, president of Kamehameha Schools; singer and storyteller Nalani Olds; and Governor Ben Cayetano.

hind the movement has been Marjorie Scott, an advertising executive who fell in love with Hawaiian music during her Island visits, which started in the 1970s. She finally moved here in 1984.

While editing a Hawaiian association's newsletter, Scott was amazed to find no archive of Hawaiian music history existed. Thanks to her efforts and those of many others, the unsung heroes of Hawaiian music will no longer go unnoticed.

Address: P.O. Box 1619
Kailua, Hawai'i 96734
Phone: 236-1517
Web site: www.hawaiimusicmuseum.org

■ MAUI OCEAN CENTER

The Maui Ocean Center, the largest tropical aquarium in the Western hemisphere, is more than a state-of-the-art fish zoo. What sets it apart? There is a strong cultural element to this marine attraction, nicknamed the Hawaiian Aquarium, which comes as a result of support from prominent Hawaiian cultural advisers such as Sam Ka'ai, Keli'i Taua, Kapi'ioho Lyons Naone and "Uncle Charlie" K. Maxwell.

Coral World International, the Maui Ocean Center's parent company, operates similar projects in Eilat, Israel and Perth, Australia. Opened in March 1998, the Hawaiian Aquarium is a tribute to the indigenous marine life of the Islands. All of its inhabitants were collected from

In the clear tunnel that cuts through this 750,000-gallon tank, visitors get a close look at a tiger shark—and vice versa. Photo by Dean Lee.

Hawaiian waters and live in habitats that resemble natural settings as closely as possible.

Maui is one of the best places in the Islands to see Hawai'i's State Mammal, the humpback whale, when it migrates here from Alaskan waters during the winter. As you participate in the Whale Discovery Center's interactive exhibits, you'll get "chicken skin" (pidgin for goose bumps) knowing pods of humpback whales may be frolicking just beyond the waters of nearby Mā'alaea Harbor.

The Open Ocean Exhibit treats visitors to a glimpse of life in the deep blue. Here, you can walk through a fifty-foot-long clear acrylic tunnel that cuts through a 750,000-gallon saltwater tank teeming with nearly 2,000 pelagic animals. Ocean naturalists are on hand daily to provide presentations on the various exhibits. In addition, there are programs for school groups, monthly "Sea Talk" evening lectures by prominent marine and Hawaiian culture experts, and special events. The Maui Ocean Center's emphasis is on education, exploration and discovery.

Address: 192 Mā'alaea Road
Wailuku, Hawai'i 96793
Phone: 270-7000
Hours: 9:00 A.M. to 5:00 P.M. daily
Web site: www.mauioceancenter.com

■ HAWAIIAN VILLAGE
POLYNESIAN CULTURAL CENTER

The Polynesian Cultural Center in Lā'ie, O'ahu consists of seven villages representing Tonga, Samoa, Tahiti, Hawai'i, Fiji, Maori New Zealand and the Marquesas. Here you can sample the food, customs, language, music, dances and history of all these South Pacific islands without boarding a plane or showing your passport.

The Hawaiian Village fills a verdant acre with seven hale (houses) that look like what Captain Cook might have seen when he arrived in the Islands. Native woods were used for framing, pili grass for thatching, and lau hala (pandanus leaves) for matting and covering the inner walls. Stones line the floor. Some of the 'umeke (wooden bowls), ipu (bottle gourds) and poi pounding boards are antiques dating back more than a century.

Don't miss the koa canoes. One is over 230 years old and the other practically "new" at 170 years. Around the wetland taro patch, the village is landscaped with thirty native plants,

The Hawaiian Village recalls life in olden Hawai'i.

including ten unique to the community of Lā'ie, which also is home to Brigham Young University's Hawai'i campus and the first Mormon temple built outside North America.

In the Hawaiian Village you can get a quick hula lesson and learn how to play the bamboo nose flute, 'ūli'ūli (feather gourd rattle), pū'ili (bamboo rattles) and 'ili'ili (small smooth stones), Hawai'i's answer to the castanets. You can watch lau hala being woven into mats and hats, taste poi while learning how taro is grown, and play traditional Hawaiian games like kōnane (checkers) and 'ulu maika (bowling).

Best of all, you'll be able to enjoy the friendly upbeat mood created by students who actually hail from the islands showcased at the center. For many, this chance to interact is the highlight of their visit to the Polynesian Cultural Center.

Students from Brigham Young University-Hawai'i form the core of performers at the Polynesian Cultural Center.

Address: 55-370 Kamehameha Highway
Lā'ie, Hawai'i 96762
Phone: 293-3333
Hours: 12:30 to 9:30 P.M. daily except Sunday.
A Hawaiian lū'au starts at 5:30 P.M.
Web site: www.polynesia.com

■ SEA LIFE PARK HAWAI'I

Sea Life Park Hawai'i is a marine-world attraction that has earned special recognition for its educational and environmental efforts. A portion of its admission price is dedicated to marine animal rescue and rehabilitation programs. Every year, Sea Life Park rehabilitates many injured seabirds, protects and studies the endangered Hawaiian monk seal, and releases newly hatched Hawaiian green sea turtles—an endangered species—into the ocean.

Endangered green sea turtles are nurtured to maturity before they're released into the open ocean.

At the 300,000-gallon Hawaiian Reef Tank, you'll feel like you're underwater, but you won't get wet. A spiral ramp encircles the tank, and windows at every level down to three fathoms enable you to admire thousands of sea creatures, including sharks, stingrays, and an occasional scuba diver sent inside to entertain visitors and feed the fish, probably in that order.

In the Hawaiian Ocean Theater—an eight-foot-high glass tank—you can watch dolphins perform both above and below the water. The Dolphin Cove is another place to see these amazing mammals display their grace and intelligence under the direction of a park trainer.

Among Sea Life Park's newer interactive adventures are Splash U and Dolphin Adventures. During their up-close and personal experience with the dolphins, participants learn how professional trainers elicit certain behaviors from them. At Sea Life Park, visitors also can feed and swim with stingrays and embark on a thrilling underwater photo "safari" in the Hawaiian Reef Tank.

These programs include park admission and are truly unforgettable experiences, especially for teenagers. Be sure to call ahead to confirm times and make reservations. And be sure you meet Kekaimalu, the world's only known "wholphin"—a cross between a bottlenose dolphin and a false killer whale.

Dolphins are the stars, and people the supporting cast, at Sea Life Park.

Address: 41-202 Kalaniana'ole Highway
Waimānalo, Hawai'i 96795
Phone: 259-7933
Hours: 9:30 A.M. to 5:00 P.M. daily
Web site: www.sealifeparkhawaii.com

■ WAIKĪKĪ AQUARIUM

Founded in 1904, the Waikīkī Aquarium is the third-oldest public aquarium in the nation. It was built by the Honolulu Rapid Transit Authority to lure passengers to ride to the end of its new Waikīkī trolley line.

Today, the Aquarium is administered by the University of Hawai'i and belongs to a national partnership of elite aquariums designated as Coastal Ecosystem Learning Centers. Located on the Waikīkī shoreline beside a living reef that's a marine life sanctuary, the small, 2.35-acre site has an impact beyond its size. Its exhibits, programs and research focus on the coral reef life of Hawai'i and the tropical Pacific. Over 2,000 aquatic creatures live here, representing 400 species ranging from corals of every shape and color to delicate sea jellies, beautiful reef fish, the endangered Hawaiian monk seal and more.

Known as the "best small aquarium" in the United States, the Waikīkī facility boasts some big achievements, including being the first to

Over 2,000 aquatic species, from common to quite rare, are displayed in this amazing aquarium.

hatch the deep-water chambered nautilus in captivity. As a center for conservation awareness, it teaches reef protection to tens of thousands of people each year, and participates in events like Make A Difference Day, when thousands of volunteers nationwide turn out to care for the community and the environment.

Intimate settings allow visitors to get eye-to-eye with marine life. One fascinating exhibit demonstrates that corals are really alive! Another shows how early Hawaiians used marine animals and ocean resources in their everyday lives. And, at the outdoor Edge of the Reef exhibit, trained volunteers lead up-close encounters with reef and tidepool creatures.

Address: 2777 Kalākaua Avenue
Honolulu, Hawai'i 96815
Phone: 923-9741
Hours: 9:00 A.M. to 5:00 P.M. daily except
Christmas Day
Web site: www.waquarium.org

Set on a parcel of valuable oceanfront land, Waikīkī Aquarium adjoins a protected living reef.

No visit to Hawai'i is complete without experiencing at least one lū'au. Shown here are hula dancers at Maui's Old Lahaina Lū'au.

The Old Lahaina Lūʻau is considered to be
among the best in the state.

No visit to Hawaiʻi is complete without a generous sampling of Hawaiian music, which offers both entertainment and a guide to the culture. Sure, you can find great Las Vegas-style revues, discos, magic shows, tea dances, rock and even jazz in the Islands. But nowhere else can you find the same quality and quantity of Hawaiian music—if you know where to look.

Hawaiian music comes out of a wonderful tradition that started with chants and hula. To this was added the pious strains of hymns that the missionaries brought from New England and the refrains of Spanish vaqueros brought to the Islands to herd cattle and teach the Hawaiians to be cowboys.

The ancient Hawaiians had drums, rattles and nose flutes. Portuguese immigrants who came to work on Island sugar plantations brought a little stringed instrument called the *braguinha* with them. The Hawaiians dubbed this instrument ʻukulele, or jumping flea, which described how the fingers of Portuguese musicians looked as they quickly plucked the strings. Island musicians tuned the vaqueros' guitars in a looser way, creating a whole new sound that's known today as kī hōʻalu or "slack key."

Hawaiian music always responds to the outside world. When rock was king, local music answered with stronger rhythms. When Caribbean reggae was popular, a sound called Jawaiian (Jamaican-Hawaiian) was born. Country and western has been a regular inspiration, a tradition reinforced by the Hawaiians' frequent use of the acoustic and the pedal steel guitar.

Through all this, hula and chant have been the constant. Nineteenth-century missionaries tried to stamp out hula, and nearly succeeded. What had been a deeply spiritual art form was nearly extinguished because the prudish New Englanders thought it lascivious. King Kalākaua, affectionately known as the Merrie Monarch, is credited with reviving the hula. Today, as the Hawaiian language and culture have undergone a renaissance, so have Hawaiian music and dance.

The shows described here run the gamut, from the quaint Pleasant Hawaiian (formerly Kodak) Hula Show to ʻUlalena, the most imaginative and innovative local entertainment in decades. In between are a variety of lūʻau shows. You will no doubt find something to enjoy.

■ ALIʻI LŪʻAU

POLYNESIAN CULTURAL CENTER

The Polynesian Cultural Center, Hawaiʻi's number-one paid visitor attraction, is located on forty-two acres of Oʻahu's verdant North Shore. Nestled in a tropical setting, this educational theme park allows visitors to experience the culture and beauty of seven Polynesian islands, including Hawaiʻi.

The Aliʻi (Royal) Lūʻau showcases Hawaiian life from the ancient days of the aliʻi through the nostalgic 1930s and '40s. Guests are welcomed with the blowing of the conch shell and presentation of shell lei. As they enter the lūʻau area, they are greeted by lush greenery and a fifteen-foot waterfall. The open-air dining area, with seating for 500, is sheltered under an enormous replica of a voyaging canoe hull. The buffet dinner features many local favorites, including kālua (roast) pig, poi and haupia (coconut pudding).

Visitors watch as a whole pig is lifted from the imu, or underground oven.

Once guests are seated, the Aliʻi Court is introduced and a hula kahiko (ancient dance) is performed. Guests are invited to gather at the imu (underground oven) to see the roasted pig lifted off steaming rocks. The lūʻau culminates with an entertaining show featuring classic songs and dances like "Pearly Shells."

The Polynesian Cultural Center was founded by the Church of Jesus Christ of Latter-day Saints to support students from around the world attending neighboring Brigham Young University-Hawaiʻi. Many of these students come from the Pacific Islands represented at the Center and enjoy sharing a real part of their home with visitors.

Address: 55-370 Kamehameha Highway
Lāʻie, Hawaiʻi 96762
Phone: 293-3333
Hours: 12:30 to 9:30 P.M. daily except Sunday.
The Aliʻi Lūʻau starts at 5:00 P.M.
Web site: www.polynesia.com

Every guest receives a lei at the Aliʻi Lūʻau.

■ DRUMS OF PARADISE
HYATT REGENCY KAUA'I RESORT & SPA

How does a lū'au show from Kaua'i get into the *Guinness Book of Records?* Doing the "world's coldest hula" at eighteen degrees below zero. That's one claim to fame of Drums of Paradise, the award-winning show at the Hyatt Regency Kaua'i Resort & Spa.

Lovely hula hands tell the tales
of old Hawai'i.

On a tour a few years ago to Minnesota, the troupe arrived in Minneapolis-St. Paul on the coldest day of the season. Most of the young people from Kaua'i had never even *seen* snow, much less danced in it.

That did not stop twenty-five barefooted dancers in lavalavas and coconut-shell bras from performing at the Hyatt Regency Minneapolis, the Mall of America and amid falling snowflakes on the roof of a Minneapolis television station. The promotion was a sensation in the snow-packed Twin Cities, which ranks number six among Hawai'i's top ten Mainland visitor markets.

Led by producer Gus Lactaoen, Drums of Paradise performers have been featured on the "Regis & Kathie Lee" television show. At home, they've entertained Hollywood luminaries who've come to Kaua'i to make films, including Steven Spielberg, Jeff Goldblum, John Travolta and his wife, Kelly Preston, who grew up on O'ahu. Even Tiger Woods has taken a break from swinging on the golf course to enjoy watching hula dancers doing their own bit of swinging onstage.

But Drums of Paradise is not all about celebrities. This show is famous for making everyone feel a party of the same 'ohana or family. Once, cast members participated in a wedding ceremony onstage for an elderly Alabama couple, childhood sweethearts whose spouses had both passed away.

The strength of their hula traditions is safeguarded by veteran kumu hula (hula teacher) Ku'ulei Punua and the Hyatt Regency Kaua'i Resort & Spa's Hawaiiana Council. Shows include arts and crafts displays and highlight the historic and legendary connection between Hawai'i and Tahiti.

Address: 1571 Po'ipū Road
Kōloa, Hawai'i 96756
Phone: 742-1234
Hours: 6:00 P.M. Sunday and Thursday
Web site: www.hyatt.com/usa/kauai/
hotels/restaurants

■ LOBBY BAR
WAIKĪKĪ BEACH MARRIOTT RESORT

Kama'āina (Island residents) and frequent visitors sometimes lament the disappearance of Hawaiian music from Waikīkī. The truth is there is plenty.

One of the best places is the Lobby Bar at the Waikīkī Beach Marriott Resort, which doesn't have a cover charge or drink minimum. Here, the Hawaiian music is undiluted—the kind you hear in the Islands at a baby's first birthday lū'au or at a backyard gathering of friends, family and neighbors.

The mix of locals and visitors at this lounge brings back fond memories of Duke Kahanamoku's and the Barefoot Bar, favorite watering holes in Waikīkī in the 1950s. On any given night, you can hear performers such as Ikona, with their famous cha-lang-a-lang style;

Auntie Genoa Keawe, Hawai'i's First Lady of Song, performs weekly in the Lobby Bar.

falsetto virtuoso Dennis Pavao; and slack key virtuosos Dennis Kamakahi, Ledward Ka'apana, George Kuo and Martin Pahinui.

The Lobby Bar also has featured the legendary Auntie Genoa Keawe, whose career in show business spans over fifty years. She has an incredible repertoire of traditional Hawaiian language and hapa haole, or Hawaiian/ English songs, most sung in her signature sweet falsetto. Still going strong, this octogenarian is the only one in the room who's not short of breath after she sings her trademark song, "Alika."

If these names mean nothing to you, plan on visiting the Lobby Bar for real Hawaiian music in a laid-back setting. You won't be sorry.

Address: 2552 Kalākaua Avenue
Honolulu, Hawai'i 96815
Phone: 922-6611
Web site: www.marriott.com

The bar's laid-back atmosphere and reasonable prices draw locals as well as visitors.

■ OLD LAHAINA LŪʻAU

Millions around the world enjoyed a taste of Maui's Old Lahaina Lūʻau as they watched the 2000 Macy's Thanksgiving Day parade. Two dozen dancers from the show—along with Miss America, Hawaiʻi's Angela Perez Baraquio— rode a float decorated with tikis, a grass hut and a volcano spouting confetti.

The popularity of the Old Lahaina Lūʻau is no surprise. Maui folks regularly rate this the best lūʻau on the island. *Frommer's Hawaiʻi, Eyewitness Travel Guides, Hawaiʻi* magazine and the *New York Times* echo the local opinion.

What makes a lūʻau special? Not the pig, but the people. One reason for Old Lahaina Lūʻau's success is the Hui Hoaloha (Group of Friends) or employees' council, which organizes cultural and educational programs for the staff.

Now over fifteen years old, the Old Lahaina Lūʻau moved in 1998 from "downtown" Lahaina to its present location on two acres at the north

The Old Lahaina Lūʻau's ʻohana (family) works hard—and has a lot of fun doing it.

edge of town near Māla Wharf. With sunset, the ocean and the island of Lānaʻi providing a stunning backdrop, this setting seems made for hula. The show's dances and chants are researched for authenticity; in fact, the lead chanter is a kumu hula (hula teacher) who conducts classes on Hawaiian culture throughout the Pacific.

From the founders to the food servers, the 150 employees take pride in the Old Lahaina Lūʻau's setting, food and entertainment. The lūʻau draws a full house of guests virtually every night. Amazingly, its buffet feeds more than 400 people in less than half an hour, and you don't get the feeling of being crowded or rushed.

A lovely seaside setting and talented performers contribute to this lūʻau's success.

**Address: 1251 Front Street
Lahaina, Hawaiʻi 96761
Phone: 667-1998
Hours: Daily at 5:30 P.M. during the winter and 6:00 P.M. during the summer
Web site: www.oldlahainaluau.com**

■ PARADISE COVE LŪʻAU

One of the state's largest and oldest lūʻau shows, Paradise Cove Lūʻau is staged on twelve oceanfront acres on the leeward coast of Oʻahu. A venerable twenty years old, it was attracting crowds long before the deluxe Kō ʻOlina Resort—with its luxury hotel, golf course and custom housing—grew up around it.

With lush lawns, a white sand beach and a ring of palm trees behind it, the location is truly lovely. Sunsets here are gorgeous. It's no wonder companies such as Sony and the National Football League have hosted lavish events here.

Paradise Cove Lūʻau is an hour's drive from Waikīkī by chartered bus. In return for what some may consider a long trip, it offers the chance to see Oʻahu's less-traveled leeward coast and enjoy Hawaiian food at prices that are a bit more reasonable than equivalent hotel shows in Waikīkī.

Like many lūʻau, Paradise Cove has a net-fishing demonstration, torch-lighting ceremony, traditional Hawaiian games and a pig roasted in an authentic imu or underground oven.

Other than its setting, what distinguishes this lūʻau from its counterparts is its award-winning revue, the work of O'Brien Eselu and his dancers. Eselu, who emcees as well as produces and directs the nightly show, is the accomplished kumu hula (hula teacher) of the award-winning Ke Kai O Kahiki Hālau (troupe), which regularly wins awards at the internationally acclaimed Merrie Monarch Festival in Hilo, the Olympics of hula competitions.

Address: 2024 North King Street, Suite 209 Honolulu, Hawaiʻi 96819
Phone: 842-5911
Hours: Buses depart select Waikīkī hotels at 4:15 P.M. and return at 10:00 P.M.
Web site: www.paradisecovehawaii.com

Paradise Cove Lūʻau's revue weaves together songs and dances from throughout the South Pacific.

■ PLEASANT HAWAIIAN HULA SHOW

The Kodak Hula Show, begun in 1937, is truly the kupuna, or grandparent, of Hawaiian shows. Started near the Natatorium as an incentive for tourists to buy more Kodak film, the show moved to the grounds of the Waikīkī Shell in Kapiʻolani Park in 1969. Three times a week, the 5,000-seat amphitheater is filled with happy visitors who pay nothing to watch the cast of talented hula dancers, young and old, perform and pose for pictures.

In July 1999, when Kodak announced it would no longer subsidize the show, it looked for a time that a venerable tradition known and loved by millions would disappear from Waikīkī. The cost to keep the show running had soared to over $500,000 a year—no small commitment.

Millions of visitors have this very photo in their Hawaiian vacation scrapbooks.

While tourism officials looked frantically for a way to keep the show alive, the Hogan Family Foundation stepped forward and saved it. Founded by Ed and Lynn Hogan, owners of California-based Pleasant Hawaiian Holidays, the foundation assumed full responsibility for the show and kept the content, staffing, schedule and even the name the same.

Eighteen months later, the show's name was changed to Pleasant Hawaiian Hula Show. Since it started as a small travel business in New Jersey in 1959, Pleasant Hawaiian Holidays has brought more than five million visitors to Hawaiʻi.

And so the show goes on. While keeping an eye on tradition, the new patrons hope to make it a venue for introducing new talent in Hawaiian music and fashion.

Address: Waikīkī Shell, Kapiʻolani Park
2805 Monsarrat Avenue
Honolulu, Hawaiʻi 96815
Phone: 945-1810
Hours: 10:00 A.M. Tuesday,
Wednesday and Thursday

■ TRADITIONS AT KAHALU'U
OHANA KEAUHOU BEACH RESORT

One of Hawai'i's newest lū'au shows is the OHANA Keauhou Beach Hotel's Traditions at Kahalu'u. To create its lū'au show, the Big Island resort enlisted noted historian and kumu hula (hula teacher) Nani Lim Yap and her dance troupe, Na Lei O Kaholokū Hālau.

Yap grew up learning the hula and Hawaiian culture on the very site that the hotel now occupies on the shores of Kahalu'u Bay. She has put together a presentation that is uncompromisingly authentic, from the entertainment to the cultural presentations to the preparation of the food.

Respected Big Island historian and kumu hula (hula teacher) Nani Lim Yap and her hālau (troupe) headline the Traditions at Kahalu'u show.
Photo by Charla Thompson.

As you enter the lū'au grounds in the coconut grove next to the ocean, Hawaiian music fills the air. A torch-lighting ceremony and chant tell the story of the area—historic Keauhou, a playground of royalty. King Kalākaua built an oceanfront retreat here; a replica of the modest cottage stands on the grounds of the OHANA Keauhou Beach Resort.

You can watch and participate in poi pounding, tapa cloth making, lau hala (pandanus leaf) weaving and Hawaiian games like kōnane (Hawaiian checkers) and 'ulu maika (bowling). The lū'au feast is traditional, starting with a Hawaiian pule or prayer. Kālua pig, fresh fish and other local delicacies are prepared according to traditional methods.

Only Hawaiian hula is performed during the evening. Some dances tell stories of how Pele, Hawai'i's fire goddess, traveled from Tahiti to Hawai'i. Her fiery displays of anger resulted in the formation of new land in her new home. Another hula talks about the life of a Kona coffee farmer who picks beans better than a machine. A third moving dance describes a royal Hawaiian wedding.

Address: 76-6740 Ali'i Drive
Kailua-Kona, Hawai'i 96740
Phone: 324-2550
Hours: 5:45 P.M. Thursday

■ 'ULALENA

'Ulalena is said to be the name of a wind peculiar to Maui. It is also the name of a show that has blown up quite a storm in the Islands.

A few years ago, entrepreneur Roy Tokujo envisioned something completely different in Hawaiian entertainment—a performance that would convey mythology and history as never before. He brought it to reality.

'Ulalena pairs the technical wizardry of ARRA Montreal, which has produced major Las Vegas shows, with Hawai'i's leading historians, musicians and dancers. It combines the meditative modern dance called Butoh with acrobatic feats of amazing strength and grace. Musically, it blends New Age riffs with the steady beat of the pahu (Hawaiian drum).

Keola Beamer and his mother Nona, who are members of one of the most respected families in Hawaiian music, served as musical consultants for the show, which employs both a high-tech surround-sound system and instruments as simple as a bamboo nose flute.

Daring, graceful acrobatics make this show a standout.

'Ulalena's story starts with the Hawaiian creation myths and subsequently covers major historical events such as the arrival of Captain Cook, the missionaries and immigrants from around the world to work on the sugar plantations. The imaginative staging, brilliant cast of over twenty performers, elaborate costuming and innovative theater techniques may remind you of *The Lion King* and other Broadway marvels.

Home for 'Ulalena is the 700-seat Maui Myth & Magic Theatre, a new $10-million, state-of-the-art facility that was built specifically for it. 'Ulalena is a mystical theater experience that leaves you with a sense of wonder, awe and even spiritual rebirth.

'Ulalena chronicles Hawai'i's history through a dramatic blend of hula, modern dance and special effects.

Address: 878 Front Street
Lahaina, Hawai'i 96761
Phone: 661-9913
Hours: 6:00 and 8:30 P.M.
Tuesday through Saturday
Web site: www.mauitheatre.com

Nohea Gallery at Ward Warehouse on O'ahu presents
a fine selection of Hawaiian arts and crafts.

Delicious Island snacks, candies and condiments are big sellers at Hilo Hattie.

"When the going gets tough, the tough go shopping." Even if this not your personal motto, chances are it rings true for someone you know. Shopping is one of the undeniable pleasures of traveling—or of staying home.

Hawai'i's people are especially proud of "made in Hawai'i" products. To the traditional aloha wear, fine wood carvings, and shell and nut lei have been added thoroughly modern wares, from Hawaiian-themed mouse pads to car seat covers decorated in Polynesian patterns. And, of course, there are delectable treats such as macadamia nut candy, mango salsa, and taro and sweet potato chips.

Over the past decade, Hawai'i's shopping experience has become increasingly more sophisticated. Among the notable Mainland chains that have opened stores in the Islands are Neiman Marcus, Nordstrom, The Sharper Image, Gap, and Borders Books, Music & Cafe. So, too, have Europe's revered names in high fashion, including Christian Dior, Chanel, Gucci, Gianni Versace and Emporio Armani.

The plethora of choices has made finding that distinctive Island store more challenging. We've discovered a few gems, which we share with you here. Some of the shops are in bustling malls; others are so off the beaten path you'll probably have to call for directions. But that's the fun of it! Explore the possibilities and you'll be pleasantly surprised at the treasures you'll find.

■ DOLE PLANTATION

Originally opened as a roadside fruit stand in 1950, Dole Plantation has grown over the years to become Hawai'i's "Pineapple Experience." "Pineapple everything, everything pineapple" sums up its wares. Candy, wine, potholders, bottle washers, keychains, golf tees, cookbooks, caps, T-shirts and aloha wear—if it's made from pineapple, about pineapple or decorated with pineapple, you'll find it at Dole Plantation. Many of the items are emblazoned with Dole's sunny logo.

There's also pineapple juice, pastries, fresh spears and DoleWhip®, a frosty pineapple dessert, for sale. You can purchase fresh-cut pineapples to take with you, or arrange to have them delivered to the airport, packed and inspected for your flight out of Hawai'i.

Dole Plantation's Pineapple Garden Maze holds the distinction of being the World's Largest Maze.

The Plantation Center features a series of building facades reminiscent of old Hale'iwa town. Here, you'll find all sorts of pineapple treats, from pineapple sweetbread to pineapple chili dogs.

Inside the store, you can learn how to pick and cut a pineapple. Outside, you can see varieties of pineapple from all corners of the Earth and learn the history of what was once considered a rare and royal fruit.

Kids love to stick their heads through Dole Plantation's pineapple figure cutouts and have their pictures taken either before or after they venture through the Pineapple Garden Maze. Recognized in the 2001 *Guinness Book of Records* as the World's Largest Maze, it covers more than two acres with a path length of 1.7 miles.

All of this makes Dole Plantation a great stop on the scenic drive between Waikīkī and the North Shore of O'ahu.

**Address: 64-1550 Kamehameha Highway
Wahiawā, Hawai'i 96786
Phone: 621-8408
Hours: 9:00 A.M. to 6:00 P.M. daily
Web site: www.dole-plantation.com**

HILO HATTIE: THE STORE OF HAWAI'I

It's reassuring to see Chinese people in a Chinese restaurant. Likewise, it's great to see local people shopping at a store that has been dubbed "The Store of Hawai'i."

Once known for its very bright aloha shirts, Hilo Hattie has expanded and improved the quality of its merchandise so it now has a much broader appeal. On any given day, you'll find Island residents browsing right alongside visitors. Nifty souvenirs run the gamut, from bucket seat covers to oven mitts, all flaunting eye-catching Hawaiian motifs. Shelves are stocked with Island gourmet food products, fragrances, stationery, books, music, videos and more.

Long known for its colorful resort wear, Hilo Hattie also offers a wide variety of gifts and souvenirs.

Launched with a single store near Kapa'a on Kaua'i in 1963, Hilo Hattie now has twelve outlets in Hawai'i, Guam and the Mainland plus an impressive Internet presence. Each year, more than 2.5 million customers (one in four visitors to Hawai'i) walk into a Hilo Hattie store—and usually walk out with a bulging bag of purchases.

The world's largest manufacturer of Hawaiian, resort and casual fashions, Hilo Hattie produces more than one million garments a year. The prints of the past have been retired in favor of contemporary patterns and fresh designs.

Wearing her signature holokū (long seamed dress) and woven coconut leaf hat, the original "Hilo Hattie," Clarissa Haili, was a dominant figure in the Islands' entertainment scene for almost thirty years. The late Hawaiian singer and comic hula dancer gave up a teaching career to enter show business in 1939. She appeared in several movies filmed in the Islands, including *Blue Hawai'i,* starring Elvis Presley, in 1961.

Just as its namesake did, Hilo Hattie has shown it is possible to take Hawai'i to the rest of the world. It has opened successful stores in California, Arizona, Tennessee and Florida, and plans for further expansion are in the works.

Address: 700 North Nimitz Highway
Honolulu, Hawai'i 96817
Phone: 535-6500
Hours: 7:00 A.M. to 6:00 P.M. daily, year round
Web site: www.HiloHattie.com

Other locations at Ala Moana Shopping Center, Honolulu, O'ahu (973-3266); Līhue, Kaua'i (245-4724); Lahaina Shopping Center, Lahaina (667-7911) and Pi'ilani Village, Kīhei, Maui (875-4545); adjacent to the Prince Kūhiō Mall, Hilo (961-3077) and adjacent to Lanihau Shopping Center, Kona, Big Island (329-7200).

■ KAMEHAMEHA GARMENT COMPANY

Kamehameha Garment Company's colorful aloha shirts enable you to wear a bit of Hawaiian history, for they are reproductions of vintage designs from the 1930s and '40s. When the company opened in Honolulu in 1936, it was Hawai'i's first ready-to-wear manufacturer of the aloha shirt and the first local garment firm to win a design patent. Business was brisk at first, but by the mid-1980s, fashion was going in another direction and the company had stopped making its distinctive patterns.

In 1994, longtime fashion manufacturer Brad Walker purchased the rights to the Kamehameha Garment Company. He revived the classic prints of the original aloha shirts, using quality old-style details like coconut buttons and double-sided seams.

After the wholesale business took off, Walker opened a retail shop at Ward Centre on O'ahu, and today his nostalgic designs are among the most popular in the Islands. Many celebrities have purchased them for personal use or worn them for appearances in movies, television shows and commercials. The list of luminaries includes Robin Williams, Chevy Chase, John Travolta, Mick Jagger, Sammy Hagar, Michelle Pfeiffer, Jimmy Buffet and the Mākaha Sons, a top local musical trio. When

Kamehameha Garment Company specializes in vintage-style aloha shirts.

you're in the shop, ask to see the shirt that was made especially for Hawai'i-born sumo champion Akebono (Chad Rowan); it's a sumo size eight XL.

Kamehameha Garment Company was recently selected by the annual *Forbes FYI* magazine as the manufacturer of one of "America's Best Fifty Products." If its striking traditional patterns and bold colors are not enough to help you find the store, look for the life-size statue of King Kamehameha that welcomes shoppers.

Address: Ward Centre
1200 Ala Moana Boulevard
Honolulu, Hawai'i 96814
Phone: 597-1503
Hours: 10:00 A.M. to 9:00 P.M.
Monday through Friday,
10:00 A.M. to 5:00 P.M. Sunday
Web site: www.kamgarments.com

■ KEĀLIA RANCH STORE

As you drive through South Kona near the small town of Keālia on the Big Island, take a moment to visit the Keālia Ranch Store. It may convince you that time travel is possible.

The store is located in the old "cowboy" office of a working cattle ranch that's been in operation since the 1920s. Previously, the space also housed a dry goods store and gas station. The original pump still stands in the "pump house" out front.

You're as likely to run into local residents as visitors in the Keālia Ranch Store. When you line up at the shave ice machine, the youngster in front of you may be redeeming a coupon received for good grades at the local school.

The store retains its rustic appeal.

As unique as the store itself are the products it offers, including local crafts and artwork. It's a safe bet this is the only store in Hawai'i where you'll find "Hunt Pig" and "Hunt Goat" T-shirts along with Hawaiian quilt products, macadamia nut brittle and chocolate-covered coffee beans. If you wish to earn the right to wear one of those shirts, the ranch offers full- and half-day hunting tours in the nearby rain forest.

Save a few minutes to peruse the historic photos of "cowboy camps," cowpokes rounding up both tame and wild cattle, and cattle being swum out to freighters at Kupa Landing in the old port town of Ho'okena, now a state park just down the road.

If you wish to heft some heifer yourself, Keālia Ranch beef is sold direct to the public at bulk rates.

At Keālia Ranch Store, the dry goods of yesteryear have been replaced by fashionable clothing, quality arts and crafts, and more.

**Address: 86-4181 Mamalahoa Highway
(directly across Mile Marker 101)
Keālia, Hawai'i 96704
Phone: 328-8744
Hours: 9:00 A.M. to 4:30 P.M. daily except Sunday
Web site: www.kealiaranch.com**

◼ KINGS' SHOPS

Something about the starkly bare lava fields along the Kohala Coast of the Big Island inspires mortals to leave their mark on the landscape. Today, it is arrangements of white rocks on the ebony lava. In ancient times, it was petroglyphs, intriguing drawings etched in the rock by the Hawaiians, who did not yet have a written language.

The most accessible spot to see petroglyphs up close on the Big Island is Kings' Shops, located in the Waikoloa Beach Resort. The shopping mall hugs a section of the King's Trail, a path traversed by travelers in the mid-1800s. Take a tour with a guide or on your own to a field of more than 3,000 petroglyphs dating back to 900 A.D. These simple figures depict everything from historic events to family genealogies to everyday life in Hawai'i before Western contact.

Since it opened in 1991, Kings' Shops has strived to perpetuate the essence of Hawai'i. Bordering a peaceful ten-acre lake, the 75,000-square-foot shopping, dining and entertainment complex features exhibits on Waikoloa's geological history and murals depicting the life of Hawaiians who lived in the area long ago.

Its landscaping is a lush conglomeration of native and introduced plants that you can view close-up on the self-guided Hawaiian Plants Walking Tour. A free full-color brochure leads you on the walk, and explains how each plant came to Hawai'i and how they were named.

Kings' Shops also offers a regular schedule of free Hawaiian music and dance performances, as well as special events such as May Day and a ho'olaule'a (celebration) during Aloha Festivals in the fall.

Oh, yes, there's also great shopping at Kings' Shops, including Under the Koa Tree, which showcases an impressive array of locally made products. The new Royal Arcade, a 20,000-square-foot addition, houses high-end retailers such as DFS Galleria Waikoloa and Louis Vuitton, both firsts for the Big Island. Another addition, called the Royal Boathouse, is set for completion in the summer of 2002. It will feature a world-class lakefront restaurant, Hawaiian arts and crafts displays, and specialty shops.

Address: Waikoloa Beach Resort
250 Waikoloa Beach Drive
Waikoloa, Hawai'i 96738
Phone: 886-8811
Hours: 9:30 A.M. to 9:30 P.M. daily
Web site: www.waikoloabeachresort.com

Kings' Shops visitors enjoy entertainment, educational exhibits, petroglyph tours and, of course, great shopping.

■ KWILTS 'N KOA

The New England missionaries brought quilting to the Islands in the 1820s. Hawaiian women learned the "snowflake" cutting method and how to piece together scraps of fabric to make large patchworks. Naturally, they looked for designs in their surroundings, and found inspiration in the trees and flowers.

Their quilts also became ways to record history and send messages; the women transferred what was on their minds and in their hearts into this practical and decorative art form. The "Hawaiian quilt" developed its own distinctive look—a central pattern of one color on a contrasting solid base.

Just as the ali'i (royalty) tried to stamp out the Hawaiian language and dance in deference

Owner Kathy Tsark teaches traditional Hawaiian quilting at her shop.

to the missionaries, so Hawaiian quilts were at one time deemed taboo. Many old quilts were destroyed, and their patterns and stories strictly guarded by families.

Today, a renaissance of traditional Hawaiian quilting is flourishing. At the center of this rebirth is a little shop run by Kathy Tsark in the heart of Kaimukī on O'ahu. In business for ten years, Kwilts 'N Koa is one of the most complete quilting shops in Hawai'i. It offers authentic custom quilts, wall hangings and pillows as well as less traditional items such as vests, potholders, Christmas stockings and tree skirts. Quilting hobbyists also can purchase patterns, kits, videos, books and other supplies. Five times a week, Kwilts 'N Koa holds classes for anyone interested in helping this unique art form survive and prosper.

Students learn how to quilt pillows, bedspreads and other items.

**Address: 1126 12th Avenue
Honolulu, Hawai'i 96816
Phone: 735-2300
Hours: 10:00 A.M. to 6:00 P.M. Monday through Friday, 10:00 A.M. to 4:00 P.M. Saturday
Web site: www.kwiltsnkoa.com**

◼ MAMO HOWELL

What do the ʻIolani High School marching band; waiters at John Dominis and Sam Choy's restaurants; and the staffs at The Orchid at Mauna Lani resort, Hyatt Regency Waikīkī Resort & Spa, Alamo Rent A Car and National Car Rental have in common?

They all wear designs by Mamo Howell.

Manufacturing aloha wear in the heart of Honolulu is a long way from an international modeling career with Christian Dior on the runways of New York and Paris, but Mamo Howell has made the journey.

Coming from a family of quilters, she was inspired by her mother and grandmother to design. In 1978, Mamo (which means safflower, a favorite Hawaiian quilt design) founded a wholesale garment company. Ten years later, she opened a retail boutique at

Mamo's distinctive designs
are casual, yet classy.

Ward Warehouse on Oʻahu, whose entire inventory is created and produced in Hawaiʻi.

Howell has helped revive a fashion interest in the traditional muʻumuʻu, and also has designed career collections for contemporary women. She remains committed to perpetuating the Hawaiian art in her unique designs. From her trademark demitasse muʻumuʻu to a wedding dress that echoes European stylings, there is a Mamo to suit any occasion.

The Mamo Howell label is synonymous with grace and elegance. While several fashion designers also draw their inspiration from traditional Hawaiian motifs, you can spot a "Mamo" across a crowded room.

Address: Ward Warehouse
1050 Ala Moana Boulevard
Honolulu, Hawaiʻi 96814
Phone: 591-2002
Hours: 10:00 A.M. to 9:00 P.M. Monday through
Saturday, 10:00 A.M. to 5:00 P.M. Sunday
Web site: www.mamohowell.com

■ ■ MARTIN & MACARTHUR

Hawai'i has its own regional style of furniture which evolved as a result of the influences of local and immigrant craftsmen in the Islands at the turn of the century. Rocking chairs, beds, cabinets and coffee tables in this unique Island style can be found at Martin & MacArthur. All of the showrooms' fine furniture, home accessories and gifts are crafted of local hardwoods, including the prized koa.

Established in 1961, Martin & MacArthur has earned a stellar reputation for the quality of its products. Four showrooms on O'ahu and Maui showcase its exclusive line of hardwood furniture as well as the creations of over 300 of the Islands' finest artists, including museum-quality calabashes. Martin & MacArthur also wholesales picture-framing supplies and local and exotic hardwoods.

Jon Martin, the company's founder, and his partner, Lloyd Jones, have created an apprenticeship program for furniture makers, and they currently employ over fifty people in

One of Martin & MacArthur's distinctive rocking chairs.

the areas of woodworking and finishing, sales and administration.

Martin & MacArthur actively participates in many community organizations. The company also has taken a bold step in Hawai'i's koa re-forestation efforts. For these reasons, the U.S. Small Business Administration honored Martin and Jones as Hawai'i's Small Businessmen of the Year in 1999.

Address: Aloha Tower Marketplace
1 Aloha Tower Drive
Honolulu, Hawai'i 96813
Phone: 524-6066
Hours: 9:00 A.M. to 9:00 P.M. Sunday through Thursday, 9:00 A.M. to 10:00 P.M. Friday and Saturday
Web site: www.MartinandMacArthur.com

Other locations at Ala Moana Center, Honolulu, O'ahu (941-0074); Kāhai Factory Showroom, 1815 Kāhai Street, Honolulu, O'ahu (845-6688); Whalers Village, Kā'anapali, Maui (661-0088); The Shops at Wailea, Wailea, Maui (891-8866).

Beautifully handcrafted bowls and plates.

■ MAUI DIVERS' JEWELRY DESIGN CENTER

You may know that the State Bird is the nēnē or Hawaiian goose, the State Flower is the hibiscus, the State Tree is the kukui and the State Mammal is the humpback whale. But can you name the State Gemstone?

If you answered "black coral," move to the head of the line at Maui Divers' Jewelry Design Center, which is tucked away on a side street near Ala Moana Shopping Center on O'ahu.

Maui Divers discovered black coral in Hawai'i in 1958. Since then, the company has become the largest manufacturer of coral jewelry in the world, all the while carefully protecting this valuable natural resource.

The purity, high density and deep luster of Maui Divers black coral is recognized by fine jewelers around the globe. The firm maintains its high environmental standards by harvesting the coral judiciously, using the *Star II* submarine it developed with oceanographers from the University of Hawai'i. By using responsible business philosophy and practices, Maui Divers has raised awareness of ocean ecology not only locally but worldwide.

You can learn more about the company's accomplishments by viewing a free twenty-minute video and embarking on a tour of its factory and retail store, which more than two million people have visited since 1987.

Address: 1520 Liona Street
Honolulu, Hawai'i 96814
Phone: 946-7979
Hours: 8:00 A.M. to 5:30 P.M. daily
Web site: www.mauidivers.com

An assortment of beautiful, fanciful Maui Divers jewelry.

NATIVE BOOKS & BEAUTIFUL THINGS

Mark Twain, who wrote so passionately about Hawai'i, once said, "The man who *does not* read good books has no advantage over the man who *cannot* read them." Twain would have been a happy visitor to Native Books & Beautiful Things.

In addition to a fabulous selection of local titles, the store's O'ahu retail outlets in Ward Warehouse and downtown Honolulu carry locally made clothing, crafts, food products, soaps and more. They are owned and operated by an organization of twenty talented Island artists.

A visit to the book warehouse and shop on School Street in Kapālama—and especially a chat with founder Maile Meyer—reveals why Native Books is such an important community resource.

Founded in 1990, it encourages new Hawaiian authors, reprints out-of-print materials, and promotes books that are critical to increasing knowledge and appreciation of the Islands. The store stocks over 1,500 book titles with a Hawai'i focus in every conceivable category.

Native Books also identifies education programs, often in remote corners of the Neighbor Islands, that need a starter library of Hawaiian books, and solicits contributions to put "good books in good hands" at affordable prices. The company also sponsors the Aupuni (Nation) Artwall, a community gallery space at the Kapālama location for emerging Hawaiian artists, regular local literature gatherings and children's readings.

"Beautiful things" at the store's
Ward Warehouse location.

Whether they are residents or newcomers, people walk into Native Books' nurturing environment as customers and often leave feeling like family. The company's concept of service is "assisting every person who contacts us for information and making sure we can help them get to a source for the information they need, regardless of sales outcome."

Address: Ward Warehouse
1050 Ala Moana Boulevard
Honolulu, Hawai'i 96814
Phone: 596-8885
Hours: 10:00 A.M. to 9:00 P.M.
Monday through Saturday,
10:00 A.M. to 5:00 P.M. Sunday
Web site: www.nativebookshawaii.com
(books only)

Other locations at 222 Merchant Street,
Suite 101, Honolulu, O'ahu (599-5511);
1244 North School Street, Honolulu,
O'ahu (845-8949).

■ NOHEA GALLERY

Nohea is a Hawaiian word that means beautiful.

O'ahu's aptly named Nohea Gallery is a locally owned family business that prides itself on being a home for the most beautiful work of over 450 artists and craftspeople, four out of five of whom live and work in Hawai'i.

Original paintings and prints; fine furniture shaped from polished native hardwoods; exquisite koa wood boxes and bowls; gorgeous handcrafted jewelry; and decorative and functional glass, textiles and ceramics are among the items in its impressive inventory.

The gallery is committed to authenticity, quality and fair value. Markups are low; in fact, customers are often surprised to find prices not much higher than at craft fairs or the artists' own studio sales. This is the place to find a special gift to mark a special occasion, whether it be a birthday, wedding, new job, new home or new baby.

Nohea Gallery carries the work of over 140 talented artists and craftspeople.

Address: Ward Warehouse
1050 Ala Moana Boulevard
Honolulu, Hawai'i 96814
Phone: 596-0074
Hours: 10:00 A.M. to 9:00 P.M. Monday through Saturday, 10:00 A.M. to 5:00 P.M. Sunday
Web site: www.noheagallery.com

Other locations at the Kāhala Mandarin Oriental Hotel, Honolulu, O'ahu (737-8688); Sheraton Moana Surfrider Hotel, Honolulu, O'ahu (923-6644); Outrigger Reef Towers, Honolulu, O'ahu (926-2224).

Ceramic bowls are decorated with lovely quilt designs. Anthurium-shaped dishes can be used as ashtrays or for serving nuts, candy and ice cream.

■ VOLCANO ART CENTER GALLERY

Creativity erupts at the Volcano Art Center. Located in Hawai'i Volcanoes National Park, it's admittedly not just a stroll down the block for most people. But it is well worth the trip, as its quarter of a million visitors a year will attest. *Sunset* magazine has described the Volcano Art Center Gallery as one of ten "not-to-be-missed" places on the Big Island.

The gallery is housed in the first wooden Volcano House, built in 1877 and recognized on the National Register of Historic Places. Early travelers came to see Kīlauea Volcano—one of the most active volcanoes in the world and still the main reason 2.5 million visitors a year enter the national park—but the art center also is an amazing diversion. It provides a means of support for over 200 Hawai'i artists, and welcomes students of all ages, from all walks of life, to learn a new skill and discover a new talent in hands-on classes. The performing arts are showcased in plays, concerts and an annual hula kahiko (ancient hula) series.

Dietrich Varez, Kelly Dunn, Michael and Misato Mortara, Kathy Long and G. Brad Lewis are among the best-known artists showcased at the Volcano Art Center Gallery, but many gifted unknowns also are represented. Diversity is the key to the gallery's success; prices for its merchandise range from $5.00 to $10,000.

Address: P.O. Box 104
Hawai'i Volcanoes National Park, Hawai'i 96718
Phone: 967-7565
Hours: 9:00 A.M. to 5:00 P.M. daily
Web site: www.volcanoartcenter.org

The Volcano Art Center Gallery is depicted in an original acrylic painting by Don Epperson.

"The Coconut," haupia (coconut-flavored) sorbet in
a chocolate shell, is one of the specialties at
Alan Wong's Restaurant. Photo by Danna Martel.

Duke's Canoe Club and Barefoot Bar is
a fun place to hang out.

D ining out in Hawai'i has come a long way since the days of the "poi joke," which went something like this:

Setting: A hotel lū'au show.

The emcee asks his audience of tourists, "How many of you have tried poi?"

A few brave souls raise their hands.

"How many of you think it tastes like wallpaper paste?"

The same hands shoot up.

"So, how do you know what wallpaper paste tastes like? Is that a delicacy where you come from?"

Today, the Islands' food and chefs are drawing international acclaim and attention. Whether you call it Hawai'i Regional Cuisine, Pacific Rim Cuisine or Euro-Asian Fusion, the cuisine that got its start in a handful of local restaurants is now being enjoyed in New York, Los Angeles, Tokyo and many places in between. Fresh local produce, meat and fish are the inspiration for dishes that blend the best of the Aloha State's rich melting pot.

We offer a small but notable sampling of restaurants here. Their specialties run the gamut, from simple old-time comfort food—what kama'āina, Island residents, call "two-scoops rice and mac salad" cooking—to gourmet creations that rival the offerings of the best chefs in the world. Reservations are a necessity, especially for the most popular establishments. And it's also always a good idea to call ahead to confirm prices and the hours of operation.

In Hawai'i, the word 'ono can mean both "hungry," as in "I am 'ono for poi," and "delicious," as in "This poi is 'ono." Without the glottal stop, ono also is defined as a large mackerel-type fish that's sometimes called wahoo. Eating in Hawai'i can—and should be—a great learning experience and a glorious adventure.

■ ALAN WONG'S RESTAURANT

Alan Wong has been one of the pacesetters in the Hawai'i Regional Cuisine movement. The overflow crowds and numerous awards at his O'ahu restaurant attest to its phenomenal popularity.

Again and again, Island residents have named Alan Wong's their first choice for "special occasion" restaurant, based on its award-winning combination of food, service and ambience. Look around the dining room, and you'll see that two out of three guests are local.

Words don't do justice to Wong's innovative dishes, which are characteristically light, fresh, creatively seasoned and artistically presented. If you're a first-time guest, you should know Ginger-Crusted Onaga (Ruby Red Snapper) with Miso Sesame Vinaigrette is Wong's best seller. Hawai'i residents and return visitors will probably want to be a bit more adventurous. If so, start with the New Wave 'Opihi (Limpet) Shooter and go from there.

For his most recent cookbook, *New Wave Lū'au*, Wong researched how food was prepared and served at old-time lū'au—and then gave it a contemporary twist. Examine his menu and you'll see traditional dishes like loco moco (rice topped with a hamburger patty, eggs and brown gravy), 'ahi poke (raw chunks of yellow-fin tuna mixed with seaweed and onions), manapua (steamed bun filled with Chinese barbecued pork), kim chee (pickled Korean cabbage), kālua (baked in the underground oven) pig and poi elevated to a culinary art form. 'Ono, in both senses of the word.

Wong also operates Alan Wong's Pineapple Room on the third floor of Macy's (formerly Liberty House) at Ala Moana Shopping Center. In addition to lunch and dinner, it offers breakfast on weekends and afternoon tea daily except Sunday.

Alan Wong's Restaurant
Address: 1857 South King Street, Fifth Floor
Honolulu, Hawai'i 96826
Phone: 949-2526
Hours: 5:00 to 10:00 P.M. daily
Web site: www.alanwongs.com

Alan Wong's Pineapple Room
Address: Third floor of Macy's
Ala Moana Shopping Center
1450 Ala Moana Boulevard
Honolulu, Hawai'i 96814
Phone: 945-8881
Hours: 11:00 A.M. to 9:00 P.M.
Monday through Friday,
8:00 A.M. to 9:00 P.M. Saturday,
9:00 A.M. to 3:00 P.M. Sunday

The New Wave Taco Plate consists of Tamarind-Glazed Shrimp Taco, Kalbi Short Rib Taco with Papaya-Red Onion Salsa and Seared 'Ahi Tuna Taco. Photo by Danna Martel.

ALOHA MIXED PLATE

Not all the restaurant awards in Hawai'i these days go to the pricey purveyors of Pacific Rim cuisine or Euro-Asian fare. Maui's Aloha Mixed Plate is proud to specialize in the humble plate lunch, traditionally "two scoops rice," a scoop of macaroni salad and a hot entrée. The mammoth "mixed plate" usually includes three entrées—teriyaki beef, mahimahi (dolphin fish), and shoyu (soy sauce) or fried chicken.

Reminiscent of the plastic-covered menus of old-fashioned diners, the eatery's menu explains the origins of the mixed plate: "In the early days of the sugar plantations... workers gathered in the fields for their midday meal. The Japanese laborers would bring teriyaki beef with rice and pickled vegetable. Seated next to them might be their Filipino neighbors with the traditional dish adobo or perhaps a pork or chicken stew."

"The Koreans had their kal bi or marinated ribs and the Chinese a noodle and vegetable dish called chow fun. Hawaiians were known

The menu includes about twenty hearty plate lunches as well as burgers, salads and sandwiches.

for their kālua pig, roasted in an underground oven called an imu. It wasn't long before they began to share their foods with one another and the 'mixed plate' was born."

Historians may argue with this rosy picture of race and culinary relations in old Hawai'i, but there is no disagreement that Aloha Mixed Plate serves excellent plate lunches in mini, regular and jumbo sizes.

Maui residents have voted Aloha Mixed Plate's plate lunches as the best on the island, and the 1999 Taste of Lahaina competition singled out its coconut prawns as the "best appetizer."

The owners of the neighboring Old Lahaina Lū'au created Aloha Mixed Plate from an old pizza parlor/sports bar on the water's edge near Māla Wharf. Jocelyn Fujii's book *Under the Hula Moon* was the inspiration for the restaurant's local-style design and decor.

It's laid-back and low-key all the way at this alfresco eatery.

Address:1285 Front Street
Lahaina, Hawai'i 96761
Phone: 661-3322
Hours: 10:30 A.M. to 10:00 P.M. daily
Web site: www.alohamixedplate.com

■ DON HO'S ISLAND GRILL

Walk into Don Ho's Island Grill, fronting Honolulu Harbor in Aloha Tower Marketplace, and you can't help feeling it has been around forever, just like Don Ho! With its thatched-roof bar, outrigger canoe salad bar, lūʻau-print plastic table covers, and servers dressed in aloha shirts and shorts, you're instantly transported to an earlier time—or another world.

Where else can you suck 'em up at the "Tiny Bubbles Bar?" Don Ho memorabilia is everywhere and—turn around quickly—you may catch a glimpse of an ever-young figure wearing a ball cap, dark glasses, T-shirt, shorts, slippers and a big smile that can only be the inimitable entertainer himself. The restaurant works effortlessly to re-create the "hang loose" atmosphere of Waikīkī's old Barefoot Bar and Trader Vic's, where Ho first made a big mark.

Reasonably priced family-style food is one draw (try the Maui Taro Burger if you are on a health kick). Hawaiian entertainment is the other draw. Don Ho's features a "who's who" lineup of local talent nightly in an intimate setting longtime fans of Island music will love.

With its nostalgic look, this Oʻahu restaurant is a magnet for television cameras; it has been featured on CNN's "Travel Now" and MTV's "Real TV" as well as numerous live radio, television and Web broadcasts.

"Where Every Day is a Weekend" is the motto of Don Ho's Island Grill. And, after all, everyone knows weekends are meant for fun.

Address: Aloha Tower Marketplace
1 Aloha Tower Drive
Honolulu, Hawaiʻi 96813
Phone: 528-0807
Hours: Regular menu service is from
10:00 A.M. to 10:00 P.M. daily (reservations are
recommended at night). Entertainment goes
on until 1:00 A.M. Fridays and Saturdays,
with appetizers served from 10:00 to 11:00 P.M.
Thereafter, only drinks are served.
Web site: www.donho.com

At Don Ho's Island Grill, you may see the "Tiny Bubbles" king himself at the bar. Photo by Olivier Koning ©2000 FilmWorks Ltd.

■ ■ DUKE'S CANOE CLUB AND BAREFOOT BAR

In addition to being a superb surfer and Olympic swimmer, Duke Kahanamoku was the unofficial "Mayor of Waikīkī." You get the feeling he would have been right at home at Duke's Canoe Club at the Outrigger Waikīkī Hotel on O'ahu.

Right on the beach where the original Outrigger Canoe Club once stood, the restaurant boasts unobstructed views of Diamond Head and the ocean Kahanamoku loved. While you wait for a table, peruse the exhibit of more than 150 historic photos and forty classic posters, vintage aloha shirts, an antique koa wood canoe and paddles plus Kahanamoku's personal surfboards that were collected for Duke's by the late Hawai'i waterman and historian Tommy Holmes.

Duke's offers concerts on the beach on Friday, Saturday and Sunday afternoons, and the Liliko'i Sisters often stroll among the tables at dinnertime, performing Hawaiian classics. The Barefoot Bar is a see-and-be-seen place for the beautiful people of Waikīkī—visitors and locals alike.

Another nice touch is a traditional lei stand, the kind that once lined Kalākaua Avenue. The beauty and fragrance of fresh flowers add to the restaurant's charming decor, which

Thatched walls, rattan furniture and a nostalgic collection of memorabilia revolving around the beloved "Mayor of Waikīkī" set the mood at Duke's.

includes almost 15,000 board feet of koa plus lau hala (pandanus leaf), bamboo, peeled rattan plaiting and natural stone floors.

Oh, yes, Duke's also serves wonderful food, from a kitchen overseen by Peter Merriman, one of the originators of Hawai'i Regional Cuisine. Prices are reasonable, and local fresh fish, Big Island pork ribs and hulihuli chicken that's been cooked on a revolving spit are among the favorites.

Another Duke's Canoe Club is located at the Kaua'i Marriott Hotel on Kalapakī Bay.

Address: 2335 Kalākaua Avenue
Honolulu, Hawai'i 96815
Phone: 922-2268
Hours: 7:00 to 1:00 A.M. daily
Web site: www.hulapie.com

KĀ'ANAPALI MIXED PLATE RESTAURANT

Slippers are usually left at the door in Hawai'i, but at the Kā'anapali Mixed Plate Restaurant, the slippers are on the wall. The Slippers Display, a shadow box full of footwear provided by the staff, is just one of the endearing things about this little gem at the Kā'anapali Beach Hotel, which bills itself as "Maui's Most Hawaiian Hotel."

Employees also have contributed family relics and heirlooms for the exhibits that line the walls of the eatery. For example, the Hawaiian Display includes a two-person poi board that has been in the family of Aunty Pua and the late Uncle Ned Lindsey for over 150 years. Beautiful family aprons and crocheted hot pads are the focal points of the Portuguese Display. Photos of plantation-era grandparents adorn the Japanese Display.

Most people leave their slippers at the door. Here, they are on the wall.

The Chinese Display features dishes from the beloved Golden Jade Chop Suey House that was "the" place for Chinese food in Wailuku for nearly fifty years. Other shadow boxes show off family cooking utensils (like a kau-kau—pidgin word meaning food—tin) and a bottle collection that includes some oldies from Haleakalā Dairy. Be sure to ask for the booklet that shares the stories of the displays, which give insight into the people who helped shape Hawai'i's history.

If a restaurant serves good meals at reasonable prices, chances are it'll always be crowded. Kā'anapali Mixed Plate's booths and aloha print-covered tables are packed not just with visitors, but with hotel staff, police officers and construction workers—the ultimate authorities on food.

Shadow boxes display the staff's family heirlooms and the cosmopolitan blend of Hawai'i's population.

Address: Kā'anapali Beach Hotel
2525 Kā'anapali Parkway
Lahaina, Hawai'i 96761
Phone: 661-0011
Hours: 6:00 A.M. to 9:00 P.M. daily
Web site: www.kbhmaui.com

■ MAMA'S FISH HOUSE

After years of living a storybook life sailing the vast Pacific, Floyd and Doris Christenson returned to Maui and opened Mama's Fish House in a romantic beachfront cottage set in a secluded cove past sugarcane fields on the edge of a mill town. The year was 1973, and one of the Christensons' innovations was offering fresh fish and Island produce when most other establishments were serving steak and potatoes. In 1998, *Travel Holiday* magazine called Mama's one of "Hawai'i's best-kept secrets."

The restaurant remains a delightful reminder of old Hawai'i. Its dining room is filled with tropical flowers, and Polynesian artifacts and original oil paintings decorate the hardwood walls along with autographed photos of the many celebrities who have visited. Tapa print cloths cover the tables, and the hinged windows are always kept open, allowing guests to enjoy the cool trade winds and the spectacular view through a coconut grove of waves breaking on the white sand beach. During the days, windsurfers can be seen performing amazing spins and flips offshore.

Over 100 fishermen are part of Mama's 'ohana (family). They are not only paid for their catch, the daily menu lists their names and where and how the fish were caught. Specialties of the house incorporate Hawaiian delicacies like breadfruit, the native pohole fern, roasted kukui (candlenut tree) nut and organically grown vegetables from nearby Ha'ikū farms.

Address: 799 Poho Place
Pā'ia, Hawai'i 96779
Phone: 579-8488
Hours: 11:00 A.M. to 2:30 P.M.,
4:45 to 9:00 P.M. daily
Web site: www.mamasfishhouse.com

Mama's Fish House offers great food in a great setting.

■ ▓ MERRIMAN'S AND MERRIMAN'S BAMBOO BISTRO

The first president of Hawai'i Regional Cuisine, Inc., an organization of twelve top local chefs who are credited with introducing this unique style of cooking, Peter Merriman is a familiar figure in local culinary circles. Merriman's, his first restaurant, is often called the best restaurant on the Big Island. Bright and cheerful, it's decorated with Hawaiian art and photographs of the farmers who provide the fresh meats, vegetables and fruits Merriman uses for his imaginative cuisine.

Visitors from all over the world flock to the quaint little cowboy town of Waimea—called Kamuela by both Hawaiian traditionalists and the postal service—just to eat at Merriman's. Its signature dishes include Wok-Charred 'Āhi (yellow-fin tuna), Baked Goat Cheese in Phyllo, Kahuā Ranch Lamb and Sesame-Crusted Catch of the Day.

Overlooking Mā'alaea Harbor on Maui, Merriman's sister restaurant, Bamboo Bistro, offers gorgeous views of the Kīhei coastline along with specialties such as Prime Short Ribs Braised in Black Vinegar and Star Anise, and Kung Pao "Hot and Sour" Shrimp Stir-Fried with Macadamia Nuts and Long Rice Salad. It's no wonder the *New York Times* has described Bamboo Bistro as a "magnet for foodies." Even better, on Thursday and Friday nights, you can enjoy live jazz with your dinner.

Merriman's has become a household name among those who appreciate fine food.

Meanwhile, back in his original Kamuela neighborhood, Merriman has sponsored an annual Tomato Tasting to find the best Hawai'i-grown tomato. In 2000, the contest attracted ten local farmers showing off twenty-six succulent varieties. Produce isn't the only thing he has fostered. Each year, Merriman's Culinary Scholarship provides funds for students to attend culinary school.

Merriman's
Address: Opelo Plaza
65-1227 Opelo Road
Kamuela, Hawai'i 96743
Phone: 885-6822
Hours: 11:30 A.M. to 1:30 P.M. Monday through Friday, 5:30 to 9:00 P.M. daily

Merriman's Bamboo Bistro
Address: Mā'alaea Harbor Village
300 Mā'alaea Road, Suite 300
Wailuku, Hawai'i 96793
Phone: 243-7374
Hours: 11:00 A.M. to 3:00 P.M., 5:30 to 9:00 P.M. daily

■ TIDEPOOLS

When McBryde Sugar Company announced it was closing on Kaua'i a few years ago, it meant unemployment for over 150 people. Those who decided to stay in agriculture began considering what crops they could grow to make a decent living.

David Boucher, executive chef of Tidepools at the Hyatt Regency Kaua'i Resort & Spa, met with the farmers to talk about the kinds of produce he could use, the quantities he needed, and, most importantly, the standards of quality he required.

Chef David, as he's known on Kaua'i, organized seminars enabling Island chefs, farmers and representatives of produce companies

At Tidepools, guests dine in open-air thatched huts set on a fresh-water lagoon.

to meet. The result has been a flourishing relationship that has put the freshest, highest quality Kaua'i produce on the tables of the island's premier restaurants.

Boucher's goal at Tidepools is to use Hawaiian agricultural products (especially those grown on Kaua'i) exclusively. To that end, he creates dishes that call for them. The results have been gratifying. Although Tidepools is located in a resort hotel, it has become very popular among kama'āina (longtime Island residents) and regularly wins statewide "readers' choice" awards.

Macadamia Nut-Crusted Fish with Kahlua Lime and Sweet Ginger Butter Sauce is one of Tidepools' signature dishes. Guests also love its East Kaua'i Onion Soup, Local-Style 'Ahi Poke with Togarashi Spiced Seared Scallop, and Kimo's Famous Crab Cakes with an Avocado Salsa and Passion Fruit Sauce.

Adding to the experience is Tidepools' romantic setting in thatched huts overlooking a koi-filled lagoon.

Address: Hyatt Regency Kaua'i Resort & Spa
1571 Po'ipū Road
Kōloa, Hawai'i 96756
Phone: 742-1234
Hours: 6:00 to 10:00 P.M. daily
Web site: www.kauai-hyatt.com

The spacious, airy lobby of the Big Island's Four Seasons
Resort Hualālai. Photo by John C. Russell.

The honu, green sea turtle, is the Sheraton
Waikīkī's mascot and symbol of hospitality.

Places to stay in Hawai'i cover the waterfront, so to speak—from cozy inns and bed-and-breakfasts to mega-resorts, from budget rooms to elegant suites with a butler on call round the clock.

For many people, a hotel is the proverbial "home away from home" where they expect to be coddled and indulged. For others, it is little more than a place to leave their bag and lay their head—a base camp from which constant expeditions are launched. Either way, or more likely somewhere in between, you may be looking for that special accommodation that is Hawaiian in look, service and ambience.

It is no exaggeration to say that Hawai'i, with over a century of tourism under its belt, has taught the world what a tropical resort should be. While it's true competition has grown, the Islands have honed two things that set them apart from other sand-and-sea destinations.

One is the difficult-to-define but easily recognized aloha spirit—that display of genuine hospitality that goes beyond a smile and friendly service. The aloha spirit has been called the glue that holds together the Islands' diverse peoples and opens their arms and hearts to still more strangers in their midst.

The other unique factor is the Hawaiian culture, from which the aloha spirit springs. Many resorts have become wellsprings of information that employ respected Hawaiian cultural authorities. From tours of historical sites that may be on property to demonstrations of traditional Island arts and crafts, they are working hard to preserve the legacy of Hawai'i's ancestors.

HILTON RESORTS HAWAI'I

The Hilton Hawaiian Village Beach Resort & Spa on O'ahu and the Hilton Waikoloa Village on the Big Island are true to their names. At both of these first-class resorts, you'll feel you are in an all-inclusive, self-contained "village," separated from the world around you.

Though the two hotels are quite different in terms of atmosphere and mood, they share a commitment to bringing the Hawai'i experience to guests in an entertaining, educational and exciting way.

Bright tropical flora complements the greens at the Hilton Waikoloa Village's Seaside Putting Course.

Visitors admire two striking pieces in the Hilton Waikoloa Village's multimillion-dollar collection of Asian and Pacific art.

Hula kahiko statues at the Hilton Hawaiian Village's new Kālia Tower.

HILTON HAWAIIAN VILLAGE BEACH RESORT & SPA

"Not too long ago, I thought restoring a Hawaiian sense of place to Waikīkī was nigh hopeless," wrote the late Dr. George S. Kanahele, guru of Hawaiian cultural values. "But I think the example set by the Hilton Hawaiian Village under the leadership of General Manager Peter Schall is extraordinary." (Schall is now the Senior Vice President-Hawai'i Region/Hilton Hotels Corporation and Managing Director-Hilton Hawaiian Village.)

The Hilton Hawaiian Village has earned the accolade in many ways. The hotel has a daylong program of fun complimentary activities that includes lau hala (pandanus leaf) weaving, lei making, hula, 'ukulele lessons, Hawaiian quilting and chanting taught with patience and kindness by Auntie Elsie Hummell. It has adopted a hula school, Hālau Hula O Hōkūlani, to conduct programs for visitors, especially children, and to stage the annual Keiki Hula Oni E Hula Festival, a children's festival for which the hotel provides trophies and medals for every young participant.

To honor hula master 'Iolani Luahine and Hawaiian entertainer Alfred Apaka, known as the "Golden Voice of Hawai'i," both of whom performed at the Village in the 1950s, the resort commissioned sculptor Kim Duffett to create bronze statues for the Tapa Tower Concourse. Visitors constantly stop to admire the statues and adorn them with lei.

In addition, the Hilton Hawaiian Village commissioned renowned Big Island tapa artist

Lei making is among the resort's complimentary activities.

Puanani Van Dorpe to create an exquisite piece measuring thirty-two by three feet. It was cut into two panels measuring sixteen by three feet, which are now displayed in the Tapa Bar along with replicas of tools and descriptions of the techniques used to make the tapa.

Every evening at sunset there is a free torch-lighting ceremony and hula performance around the aptly named Super Pool. On Aloha Friday, the King's Jubilee, a tribute to King Kalākaua, Hawai'i's last reigning king, is presented. This spectacular free show starts with the precision drill team work of the eight-member Village Guard and ends with a fireworks display over Waikīkī Beach.

This is just a sampling of the Hilton Hawaiian Village's ongoing efforts to showcase things Hawaiian. With the addition of the brand-new Kālia Tower, which includes an interactive cultural center sponsored by the Bishop Museum, the resort's commitment to Keep It Hawai'i no doubt will continue to grow.

Address: 2005 Kālia Road
Honolulu, Hawai'i 96815
Phone: 949-4321
Web site: www.hawaiianvillage.hilton.com

■ HILTON WAIKOLOA VILLAGE

Spanning over sixty-two acres, this is a huge resort with a fantasyland atmosphere. But since Hilton took over the property in 1993, many touches have been added that keep it rooted in a Hawaiian context.

A small reminder, but one that reaches many guests, is the "turn-down" card that's placed on the pillows at night. Each shows an artist's rendering of Pele, the tempestuous Hawaiian goddess of fire, who supposedly dwells in the Volcano region of the Big Island. On the back of each card is a Pele legend that's been researched, authenticated and simply re-told.

As you explore the expansive grounds, look for O Kēia Ka Wahi Waikoloa (This Place Waikoloa), an exhibit of photos and artifacts that bring the hotel's magnificent setting to life. The centerpiece is a Hawaiian quilt that was hand-made by Hilton Waikoloa Village employees using motifs and materials that were specially selected to represent the surrounding area.

Hale Aloha, the lovely wedding pavilion that is also used for Sunday worship services, reflects the "golden age" of Hawaiian architecture early in the last century. It features a double-pitched hip roof that provides protection from the sun and rain while allowing the windows to be left open. Note the stained-glass windows facing the sea that depict Big Island flowers. The very same blossoms can be seen in real life through the windows.

Hilton Waikoloa Village boasts one of the few Dolphin Quest programs in the United States, which allows lucky guests to become acquainted with some of its Atlantic bottlenose dolphins under the watchful eye of marine mammal specialists. Each June, Dolphin Days celebrates en masse the birthdays of these dolphins, the hotel's punahele or favorite ones.

The real party animals, however, are the visitors who come in droves to enjoy the four-day event, a highlight of which is the Great Waikoloa Food, Wine & Music Festival. Over two dozen of Hawai'i's top chefs display their culinary artistry in booths set up under the stars, and the jazz is as cool and breezy as the weather. Dolphin Days is a benefit for the Pacific Marine Life Foundation, which is dedicated to protecting whales and dolphins, and Shriners Hospital for Children in Honolulu. As part of Dolphin Days, some of the hospital's young orthopedic patients get to meet the Waikoloa dolphins, too.

Address: 425 Waikoloa Beach Drive
Waikoloa, Hawai'i 96738
Phone: 886-1234
Web site:www.hiltonwaikoloavillage.com

Hale Aloha, the wedding chapel, sits amid the splendor of the sixty-two-acre resort.

OUTRIGGER HOTELS & RESORTS

With over 8,000 hotel rooms in Hawai'i, Outrigger Hotels & Resorts is the state's largest hotel group. Two of the eight hotels on Waikīkī Beach and almost a quarter of all hotel rooms in Waikīkī are part of the Outrigger family. And there are Outriggers on every major island.

In recent years, the company has extended its reach to the Western and Southern Pacific as far as Australia. But the company's heart, as well as its corporate headquarters, is firmly rooted in Hawai'i. Outrigger properties range from deluxe full-service resorts to modest limited-service hotels for budget-conscious travelers, most of them under the OHANA (family) Hotels of Hawai'i brand.

One thing that unites these diverse properties is Ke 'Ano Wa'a, The Outrigger Way, a program that aims to bring true Hawaiian hospitality to every guest. As Dr. Richard Kelley, Outrigger's chairman, put it, the goal is that "no matter who they contact—a front desk clerk, a bellman, a housekeeper, a maintenance specialist or someone in food and beverage—our guests know they are in Hawai'i and not in Phoenix, Baltimore or New York City. That is the Outrigger edge and the reason why our guests keep coming back time and again."

Many of Outrigger's Keep It Hawai'i efforts rely heavily on "people power." Each Thanksgiving Day, as millions of Americans watch the Macy's Thanksgiving Day parade on television, they see segments of the Aloha

The lobby of the Outrigger Wailea Resort on Maui opens to the breezes.

Festivals Floral Parade, which takes place live in Waikīkī on Oʻahu in September. For over a decade, Outrigger Hotels & Resorts has sponsored the Royal Court Float, which carries Hawaiians representing the aliʻi (royalty) of long ago. More than 100 Outrigger employees donate many hours of personal time to design, construct, decorate and even drive the float, which is always adorned with an abundance of fresh flowers.

On Oʻahu, the beachfront Outrigger Waikīkī developed the Kalākaua Experience in honor of Hawaiʻi's last reigning king. This series of monthly lectures and exhibits covers a wide range of topics, including the Hawaiian language, herbal medicine, vintage aloha wear, the ʻukulele and surfing.

At the Outrigger Reef On The Beach, also in Waikīkī, Aloha Friday is a joyous event. The activity-filled program kicks off at eight in the morning with a performance by Na Leo o Kālia, a choral group comprised of hotel housekeepers,

The Outrigger Reef On The Beach's employees help visitors get into the spirit of Aloha Friday.

and ends with strolling musicians serenading guests as the sun sets.

Outrigger Reef On The Beach
Address: 2169 Kālia Road
Honolulu, Hawaiʻi 96815
Phone: 923-3111
Web site:www.outrigger.com

Outrigger Waikīkī
Address: 2335 Kalākaua Avenue
Honolulu, Hawaiʻi 96815
Phone: 923-0711
Web site:www.outrigger.com

■ SHERATON HOTELS HAWAI'I

Two of Hawai'i's oldest and grandest hotels—the Moana Surfrider and The Royal Hawaiian—are today Sheraton hotels, so it is to be expected that the company would take Hawaiian tradition seriously.

Sheraton Moana Surfrider, the "First Lady of Waikīkī," opened in 1901. It was the first major hostelry to open in the seaside resort, and made headlines again in 1989 when its owners spent $50 million to restore it to its original grandeur. The hotel's Historical Room provides fascinating glimpses of what a first-class vacation in Waikīkī was like at the turn of the century.

The Royal Hawaiian, dubbed the "Pink Palace of the Pacific" because of its distinctive color, traces its history to February 1, 1927, when Princess Abigail Kawananakoa, part of the deposed but still-respected Hawaiian royal family, signed the register as the first guest. Recent architectural improvements and renovations have restored the stately hotel's original splendor.

The stately Royal Hawaiian has been dubbed the "Pink Palace of the Pacific."

The Sheraton Princess Ka'iulani is named after one of the most beloved members of the royal Hawaiian family. Trained and educated to assume the throne, the beautiful princess died in 1899 at the age of twenty-three, six years after the monarchy was overthrown. Every October, the month Ka'iulani was born, the hotel honors her with a weeklong celebration of music, song and dance.

No one would call the 1,852-room, thirty-one-story Sheraton Waikīkī Hotel, which opened in 1971, a historic property. But it makes its Hawaiian character and commitment clear in other ways.

To protect and increase awareness of the endangered honu, or Hawaiian green sea turtle, the Sheraton Waikīkī adopted it in 1996 as its mascot and symbol of hospitality. Green sea turtles often can be seen swimming in the waters off the hotel, especially at dawn and dusk. When the hotel underwent a five-year, $20-million renovation from 1996 to 2000, the honu was prominent in the plans, from a marine tank with a live honu at the entrance to an outreach program that provides educational materials to local schools.

Opened in 1901, the Moana (center building, now known as the Banyan Wing) was the first major hotel to open in Waikīkī. It's flanked by the Diamond Wing (left) and the Tower Wing (right), built in 1952 and 1969, respectively.

The Sheraton Waikīkī also has adopted an eighty-member hula troupe, Na Mea Hula O Kahikinaokalālani, "The Hula Dancers of the Heavenly Rising Sun," which performs for visitors in return for the hotel's support. In addition, visitors can take "A Journey to Old Waikīkī," a walking tour that begins every Wednesday at 9:00 A.M. at the Guest Services Desk of the hotel. Designed by well-known Island historian and author Glen Grant of Honolulu TimeWalks, this nostalgic trip focuses on the history of Sheraton's properties in Waikīkī.

Relaxing is easy at the Sheraton Princess Kaʻiulani, which is named after a Hawaiian princess.

All of Sheraton's employees participate in Hoʻokipa Me Ke Aloha, or Professional Training in Hawaiian Hospitality, the curriculum for which was created in partnership with Kapiʻolani Community College's Interpret Hawaiʻi Department. The teachers are graduates of the University of Hawaiʻi's Hawaiian Studies Department, and instructional materials are designed with input from Native Books, a leading publisher and distributor of Hawaiian tomes. The program starts with "cultural anchors" such as the *Kumulipo*, the Hawaiian creation chant, the story of kalo (taro) and ahupuaʻa or ancient land divisions, plus over 100 Hawaiian words and phrases. Learning is a continual process; when employees have finished one section, they move on to the next.

Sheraton Moana Surfrider
Address: 2365 Kalākaua Avenue
Honolulu, Hawaiʻi 96815
Phone: 922-3111
Web site: www.sheraton-moana.com

Sheraton Princess Kaʻiulani
Address: 120 Kaiulani Avenue
Honolulu, Hawaiʻi 96815
Phone: 922-5811
Web site: www.princess-kaiulani.com

Sheraton Waikīkī
Address: 2255 Kalākaua Avenue
Honolulu, Hawaiʻi 96815
Phone: 922-4422
Web site:www.sheraton-waikiki.com

The Royal Hawaiian
Address: 2259 Kalākaua Avenue
Honolulu, Hawaiʻi 96815
Phone: 923-7311
Web site: www.royal-hawaiian.com

The Sheraton Waikīkī promotes Hawaiian music and dance in many ways, including sponsoring a local hula troupe.

■ FOUR SEASONS RESORT HUALĀLAI

The first thing that strikes you about the Big Island's Four Seasons Resort Hualālai is its understated elegance. Its series of low-rise crescent-shaped buildings mold to the landscape created by nineteenth-century eruptions from Hualālai Volcano, which forms a dramatic backdrop to the oceanfront hotel.

As you would expect of a Four Seasons hotel, the service and amenities at this North Kona Coast property are of the highest caliber. Each of the resort's four pools is different. One is a 2.5-million-gallon pond sculpted from lava and stocked with tropical fish. Here, snorkelers can frolic in complete safety.

Given the hotel's small size (only 243 rooms) and its many top-notch features—among them a Jack Nicklaus-designed golf course, eight tennis courts and an award-winning open-air spa—it might have seemed that paying great attention to Hawaiian cultural and environmental concerns would not be necessary. But the Four Seasons Resort Hualālai not only pays attention to these issues, it celebrates them.

The focal point for bringing Hawaiian tradition and values to life for guests is the Ka'ūpūlehu Cultural Center. A library of books, audio and video recordings, artwork and exhibits are the resources for its ongoing series of cultural offerings in Hawaiian lan-

Tropical elegance defines the accommodations at this seaside resort.

guage, natural history, music and hula. As part of its celestial navigation program, for example, the resort built a star compass, a round slab of blue stone marked with a sky chart in Hawaiian. Veteran canoe travelers are invited to lecture on the glorious history of Polynesian ocean voyaging.

To its credit, the Four Seasons Resort Hualālai also maintains the anchialine ponds around its property—landlocked brackish pools that are home to the endangered 'ōpae 'ula (red shrimp), ae'o (black-necked stilt) and 'auku'u (black-crowned night heron) as well as plants the ancient Hawaiians used for medicine.

Address: 100 Ka'ūpūlehu Drive
Ka'ūpūlehu-Kona, Hawai'i 96740
Phone: 325-8000
Web site: www.fourseasons.com/hualalai

■ HYATT REGENCY KAUA'I RESORT & SPA

Many consider this to be the finest resort on Kaua'i. Part of the reason is that it does so much to capture a feeling of old Hawai'i, particularly the "golden age" of the 1920s and '30s.

The resort's low-rise architecture doesn't compete with the natural beauty of its environment. Open and airy, the public areas are decorated with art deco chandeliers, Italian marble, koa wood furnishings and calabash bowls, and magnificent arrangements of tropical flowers. As you enter the lobby, Keoneloa Bay, Po'ipū Beach and the hotel's lush gardens are perfectly framed—just like a postcard.

The wood-lined corridors exhibit an extensive collection of Pacific arts and crafts, and the rooms are decorated with rattan and wicker, quilt-like bedspreads and floral prints.

The hotel's low-rise buildings are surrounded by trees and flora.

Two acres of saltwater lagoons connect the Hyatt Regency Kaua'i Resort & Spa to the ocean and beach.

Look for the brass sugarcane leaf motif that can be seen everywhere, from wall fixtures to door handles. It recalls the cane fields that once covered fifty acres where the resort now stands.

So as not to be lulled completely into "Polynesian paralysis," the Hyatt Regency Kaua'i Resort & Spa also boasts an immense playground of pools, waterfalls, rivers and saltwater lagoons that do not seem out of place even next to 500 yards of sandy beach and breathtaking oceanfront. Every effort has been made by the hotel to fit comfortably into the environment, not fight it.

**Address: 1571 Po'ipū Road
Kōloa, Hawai'i 96756
Phone: 722-1234
Web site: www.kauai-hyatt.com**

■ KĪLAUEA LODGE

Ask anyone who has visited Kīlauea Lodge near Hawai'i Volcanoes National Park on the Big Island and the unanimous opinion will be that no place in the state is quite like it. "From the moment your car turns into the driveway, you know you have just entered a very special place and the feeling gets stronger as you enter the lodge itself," wrote one frequent guest. "It is like stepping into an older, more gentle and peaceful Hawai'i. The cares are not yours for these moments; you are instead served in a loving and warm manner by a great group of people."

Built in 1938 as a YMCA retreat named Hale O Aloha, the restored lodge is famous for its Fireplace of Friendship. This massive hearth is fashioned from a collection of stones gathered from around the world (including the Acropolis) and embedded with Hawaiian artifacts like a poi pounder and kukui nut grinder.

Generous use of koa wood and local art and Hawaiian music at every turn contribute to the magic of Kīlauea Lodge, owned by Lorna and Albert Jeyte, who doubles as the chef. People, not bricks and mortar, make the lodge a memorable retreat. This is a place where a waitress overhears that a couple without a

Kīlauea Lodge dates back to 1938, when it opened as a YMCA retreat called Hale O Aloha.

rental car is about to take a three-hour taxi ride to Waipi'o Valley. Instead, the woman drives the visitors there herself, providing an insider's tips about the Big Island all along the way.

Chef Jeyte's extraordinary cuisine has won awards from *Gourmet* magazine, among others. To ensure freshness, he works with home-grown products as much as possible. For instance, the catch of the day comes from Hilo; the beef from Parker Ranch. Expect a menu with imagination; one of Jeyte's specialties is a papaya salsa and fresh ginger sauce.

Address: P.O. Box 116
Volcano, Hawai'i 96785
Phone: 967-7366
Web site:www.kilauealodge.com

■ KONA VILLAGE RESORT

Kona Village Resort is a wonderful thatch-roofed hideaway that's often been called Hawai'i's ultimate getaway. Long before mega-resorts appeared on the Big Island's Kohala Coast, it carved out its own piece of paradise and has remained true to its vision.

Each of its "rooms" is a thatched-roof hale (cottage) in the style of the islands of the Pacific: Tahiti, Fiji, New Zealand, New Hebrides, Samoa, Palau, the Marquesas and, of course, Hawai'i. The bungalows line a secluded beach and surround an ancient fishpond.

Some of the hale, in fact, are built on the foundations of the historic Hawaiian fishing village of Ka'ūpūlehu, where as many as 15,000 Hawaiians lived before Captain Cook arrived. The resort's ambience mirrors old Hawai'i; there are no televisions, telephones or radios in any of the hale, nor are there locks on

You can really get away from it all at Kona Village; there are no televisions, telephones or radios in any of its cottages.

the doors. A coconut placed in front of your cottage serves as your "Do Not Disturb" sign.

So how do you pass your time here? Just as the ancient Hawaiians did, of course. Try making a lei or weaving a toy out of coconut fronds. Go fishing, sailing and swimming. Enjoy a nature walk or guided tour of Ki'i Pōhaku O Ka'ūpūlehu, one of the best petroglyph sites in Hawai'i. Viewing the intriguing 440 drawings of turtles, humans, paddles, canoe sails and more has become even easier since the resort added a 700-foot boardwalk of native 'ōhi'a and fir.

Address: P.O. Box 1299
Kailua-Kona, Hawai'i 96745
Phone: 325-5555
Web site: www.konavillage.com

Sailing, snorkeling, swimming—the ocean is an irresistible lure.

■ MOLOKA'I RANCH LODGE

When Moloka'i Ranch opened the first of its eco-tourism camps in early 1997, it was a way to "rough it" in comfort. Set by the beach or atop hillsides, each "tentalow," essentially a tent mounted on a wooden platform, was equipped with solar power, running water, private baths and real beds.

In 1999, the luxurious two-story Moloka'i Ranch Lodge expanded the accommodations options for visitors. Nestled on eight acres near the entrance to historic Maunaloa town, the lodge is reminiscent of a ranch house; in fact, its decor incorporates ranch memorabilia like saddles and branding irons as well as historic paniolo (cowboy) photos. Founded over a century ago, Moloka'i Ranch has a history as a cattle ranch and pineapple plantation. Although the ranch still raises cattle, most of its 54,000 acres (nearly one-third of the island) is now devoted to tourism-related activities such as horseback riding, mountain biking and cultural walks.

Horses can take you where no other mode of transportation can.

The lodge's magnificent Great Room features a painting of the enchanting Tootsie Notley, a famed hula dancer and performer of the 1930s who personified Hawai'i to many visitors. The Paniolo Lounge is decorated with photos from the Cooke family, longtime Moloka'i residents who once owned the ranch.

Each of Moloka'i Ranch Lodge's twenty-two guest rooms is decorated in its own unique style. And to satisfy its upscale clientele, it features luxurious touches never thought of in its ranching or plantation days, such as a fitness center, heated pool and spa. Other amenities include a library, game room and a wrap-around veranda that opens to stunning views of pastureland, the Pacific and, at night, the twinkling lights of Honolulu.

Mountain biking along Moloka'i's rugged north shore.

Address: P.O. Box 259
100 Maunaloa Highway
Maunaloa, Hawai'i 96770
Phone: 552-2741
Web site: www.molokai-ranch.com

OLD WAILUKU INN AT ULUPONO

The Old Wailuku Inn at Ulupono was built in 1924 by a wealthy Island banker as a wedding gift for his daughter-in-law. This queen of old Wailuku homes was restored and opened as a bed-and breakfast in 1997 by Janice and Tom Fairbanks, who share backgrounds in the hospitality industry and a love for Hawaiian history.

The decor of the Old Wailuku Inn revolves around Don Blanding, a prolific writer who produced most of his work during the 1920s and '30s. Each of the inn's seven distinctive guest rooms is dedicated to a flower mentioned in Blanding's book, *In An Old Hawaiian Garden*—Bird of Paradise, Mokihana, Lokelani, Hibiscus, Lehua, 'Ilima, and 'Ulu, the sumptuous master suite. The 'ulu or breadfruit tree flourishes on the property, and is said to repre-

'Ulu, or breadfruit, is the theme of the master suite.
Photo by Ric Noyle.

sent growth and vitality. Beds are covered with hand-sewn Hawaiian quilts displaying the room's theme flower.

All the rooms have private baths with a phone. Some have original fixtures, while others are equipped with whirlpools. Common areas reveal Janice Fairbanks' passion for Asian and Pacific art. Her numerous forays to local antique shops and estate sales have yielded a trove of decorative accents for the inn, including tansu chests, koa wood calabashes and a complete set of Blanding's books about Hawai'i—all seventeen of them.

Address: 2199 Kahoʻokele Street
Wailuku, Hawaiʻi 96793
Phone: 244-5897
Web site: www.mauiinn.com

The inn's veranda overlooks a flourishing garden.
Photo by Ric Noyle.

■ RADISSON KAUA'I BEACH RESORT

When the Kaua'i Beach Resort became a Radisson in 2000, the new owners launched a $10-million renovation, elevating the 341-room property from a two- to three-star AAA (American Automobile Association) rating. Wimberly Allison Tong & Goo, a Hawai'i architectural firm that has designed major resorts around the world, was called on to create something special for the still moderately priced resort.

For over 100 years in the Islands, most plantation families lived in simple, single-wall, wood-frame buildings. You can still see these plantation cottages in rural areas around the state. Occasionally, you also can see a grander version of this style of home, which may have belonged to the plantation manager or owner.

For the Radisson Kaua'i Beach Resort, the architects set out to capture the understated elegance of a plantation owner's home, from the inviting entryway to the spacious lobby that exudes the comfortable feeling of a living room.

The hotel uses white-gloss board-and-batten paneling on walls and ceilings. To enhance a feeling of the past, the artwork selected was archival prints. Throughout the resort, you'll see fine examples of pahu (drums) and feather lei and capes. Images of the mokihana berry

The bright, comfortable Game Room of the recently renovated Radisson Kaua'i Beach Resort.

(Kaua'i's official flower), maile leaves and ferns accent public and private spaces. The carpets are patterned after lau hala (pandanus leaves), and triple-strand kukui nut leis hold back the drapes in the rooms.

The twenty-five-acre resort is lushly landscaped with tropical plants and flowers, cascading waterfalls and a dramatic rock pool by the sea. In short, it's an environment that exudes the beauty of Hawai'i and its laid-back lifestyle.

Address: 4331 Kaua'i Beach Drive
Līhue, Hawai'i 96766
Phone: 845-1955
Web site: www.radisson.com

NOTES